# ADULT COLORING BOOK DESIGNS

## A HUGE ADULT COLORING BOOK OF 60 DETAILED AND INTRICATE STRESS RELIEF DESIGNS

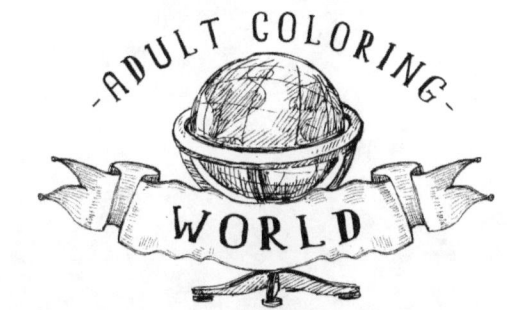

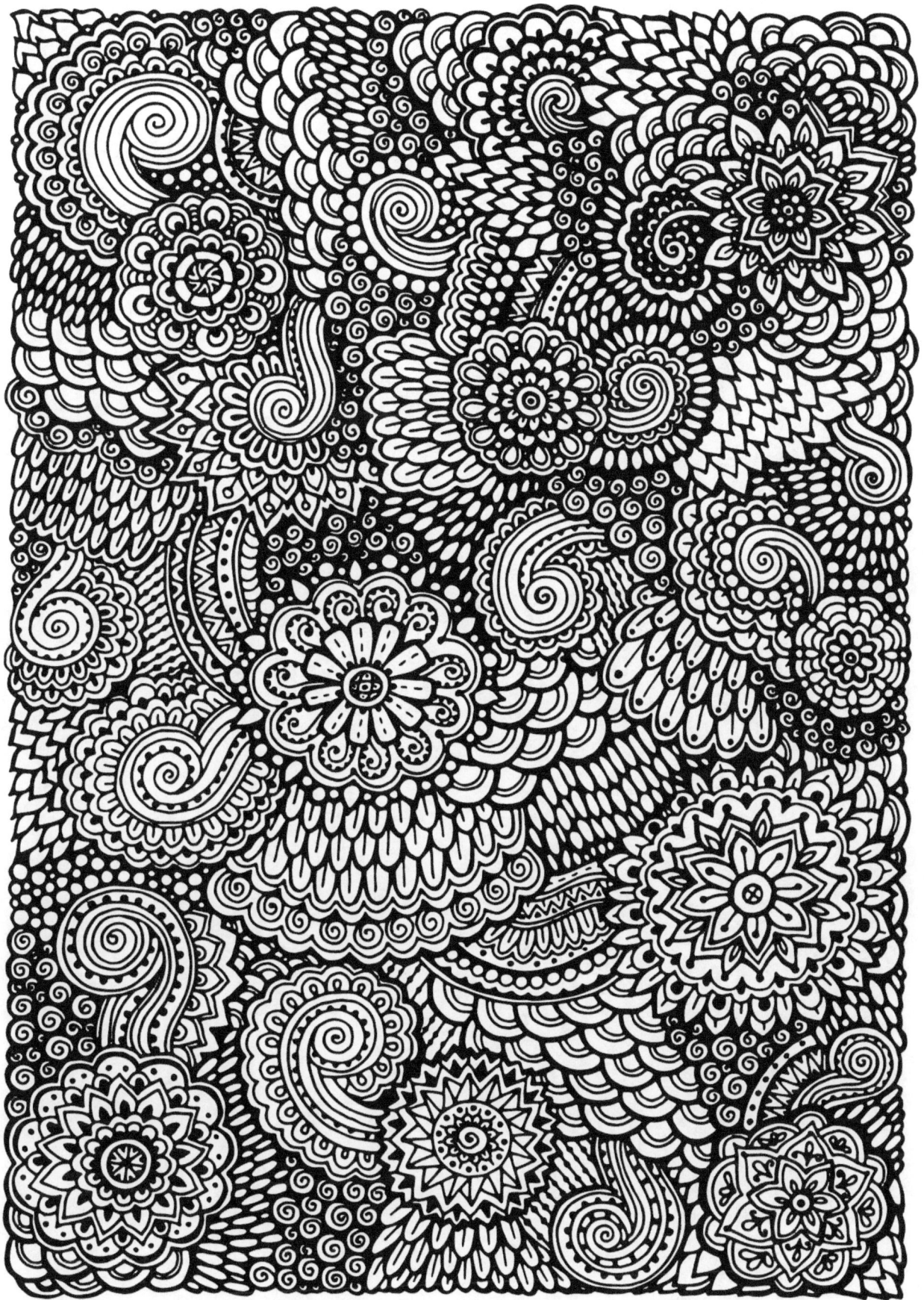

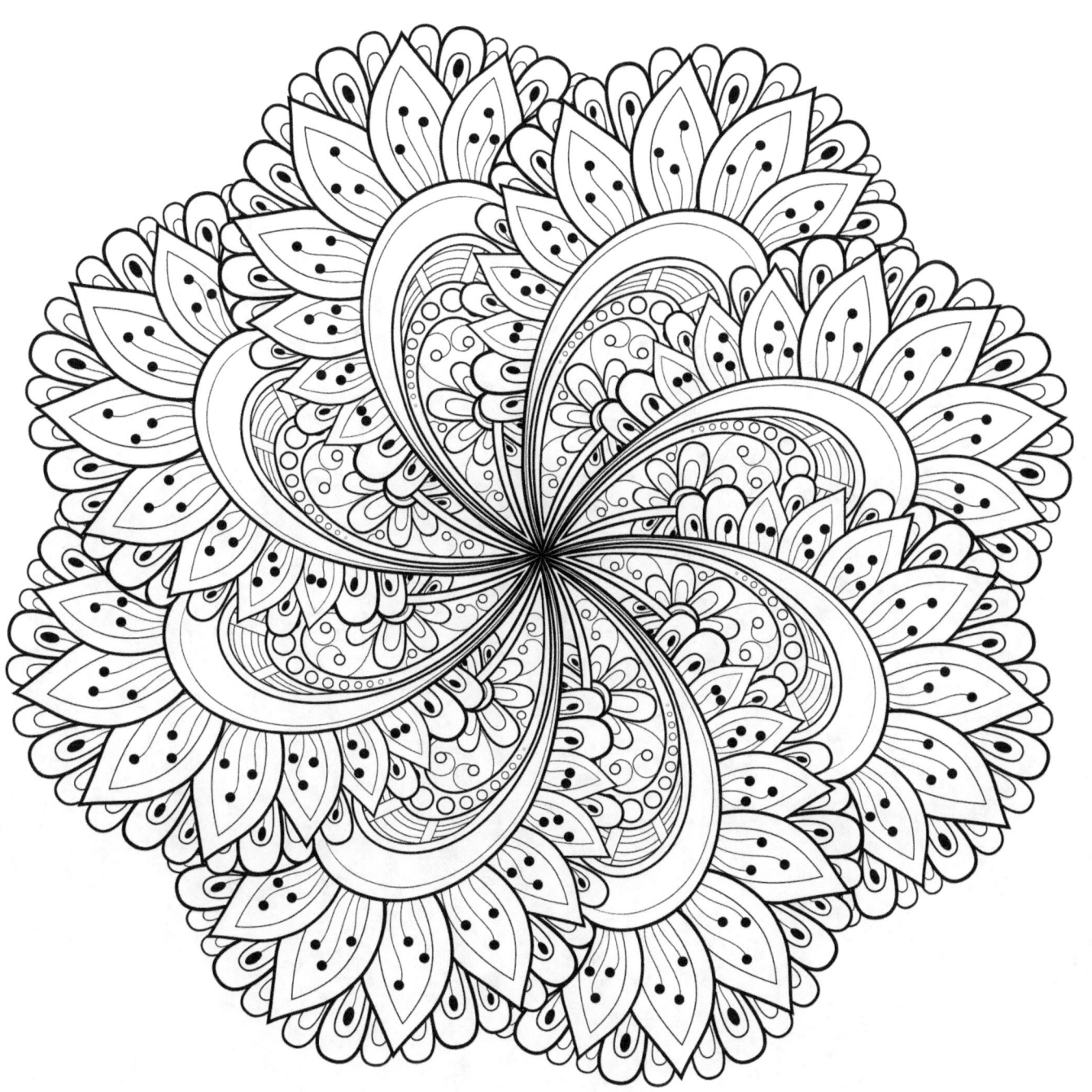

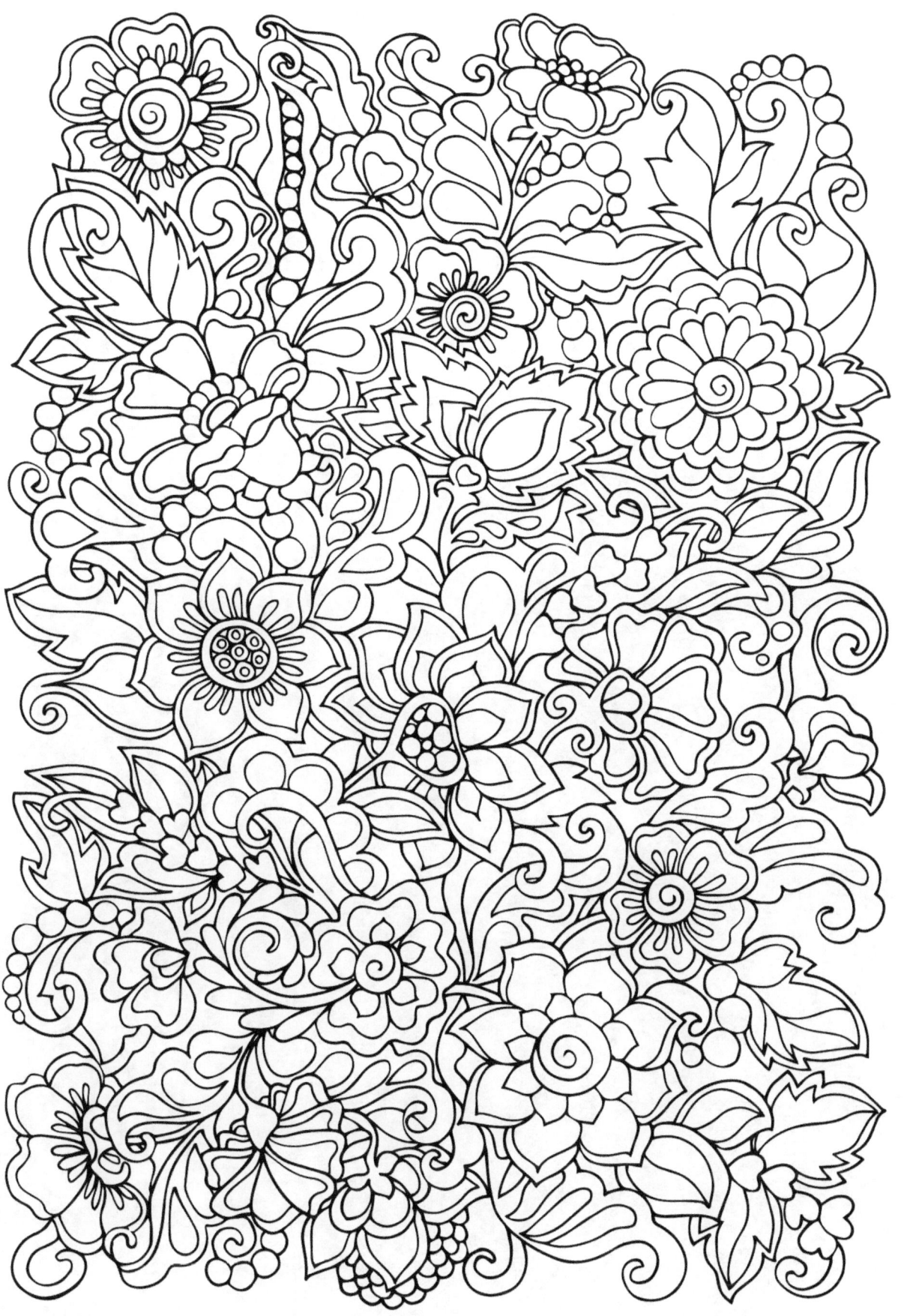

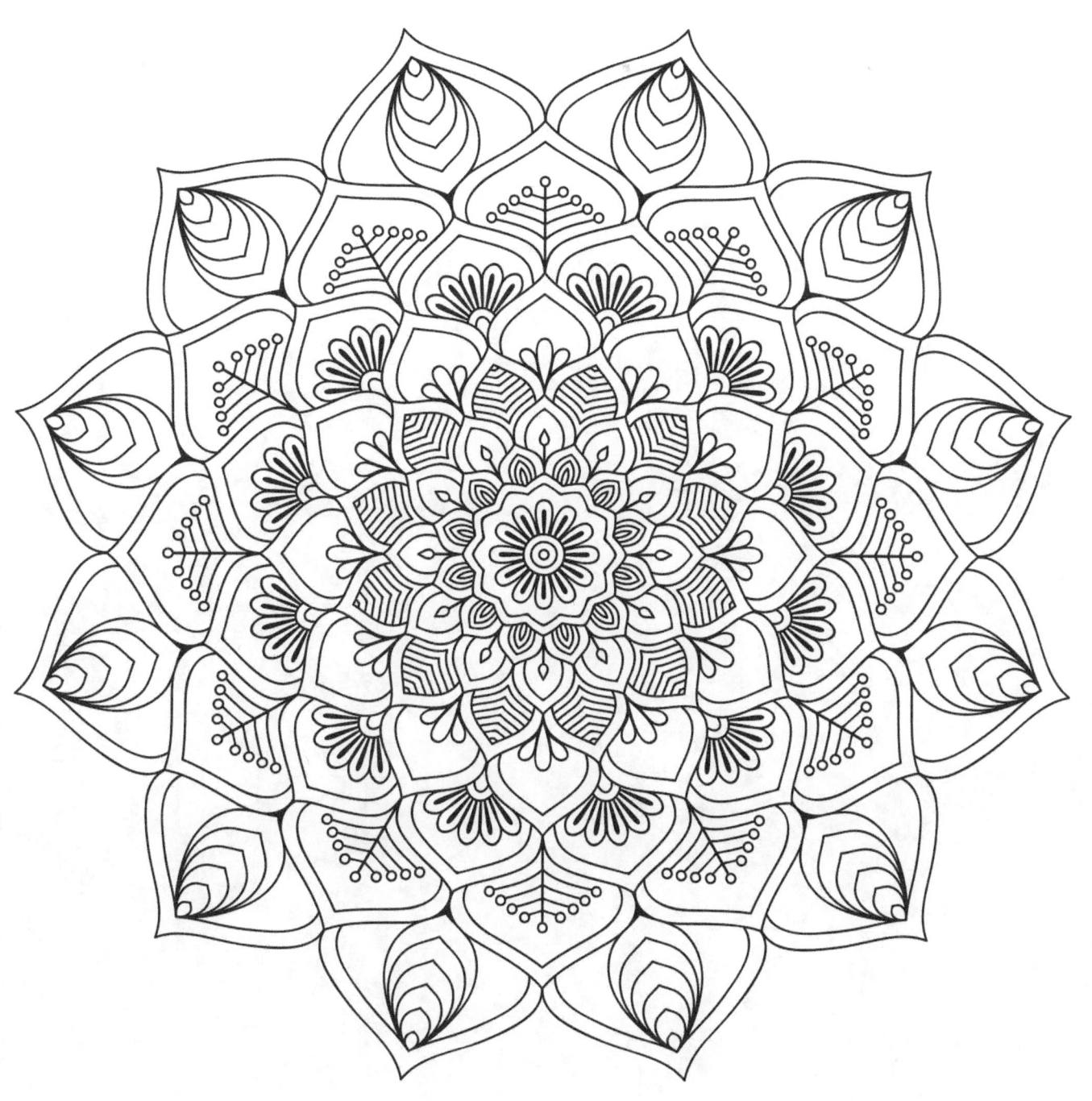

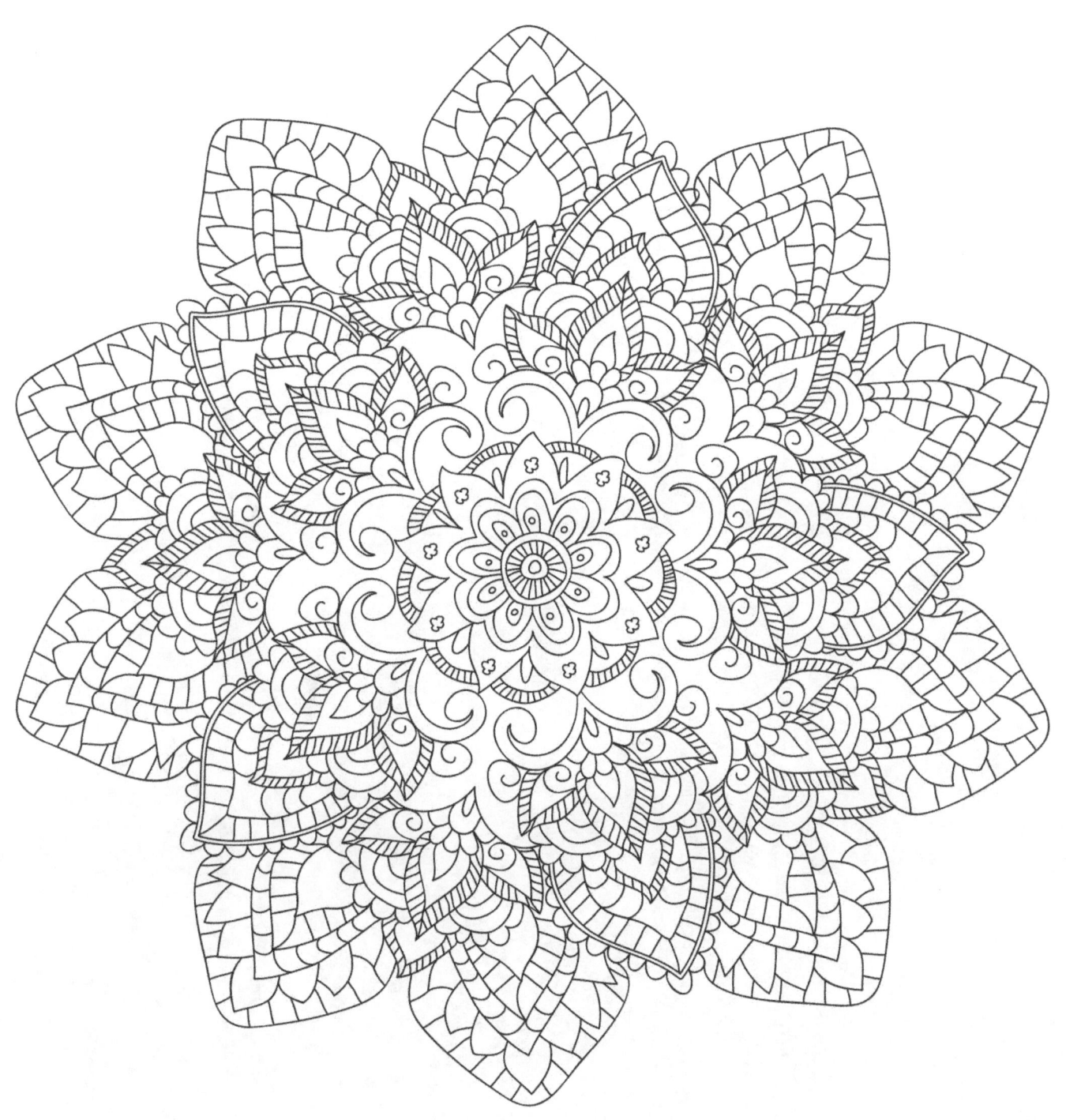

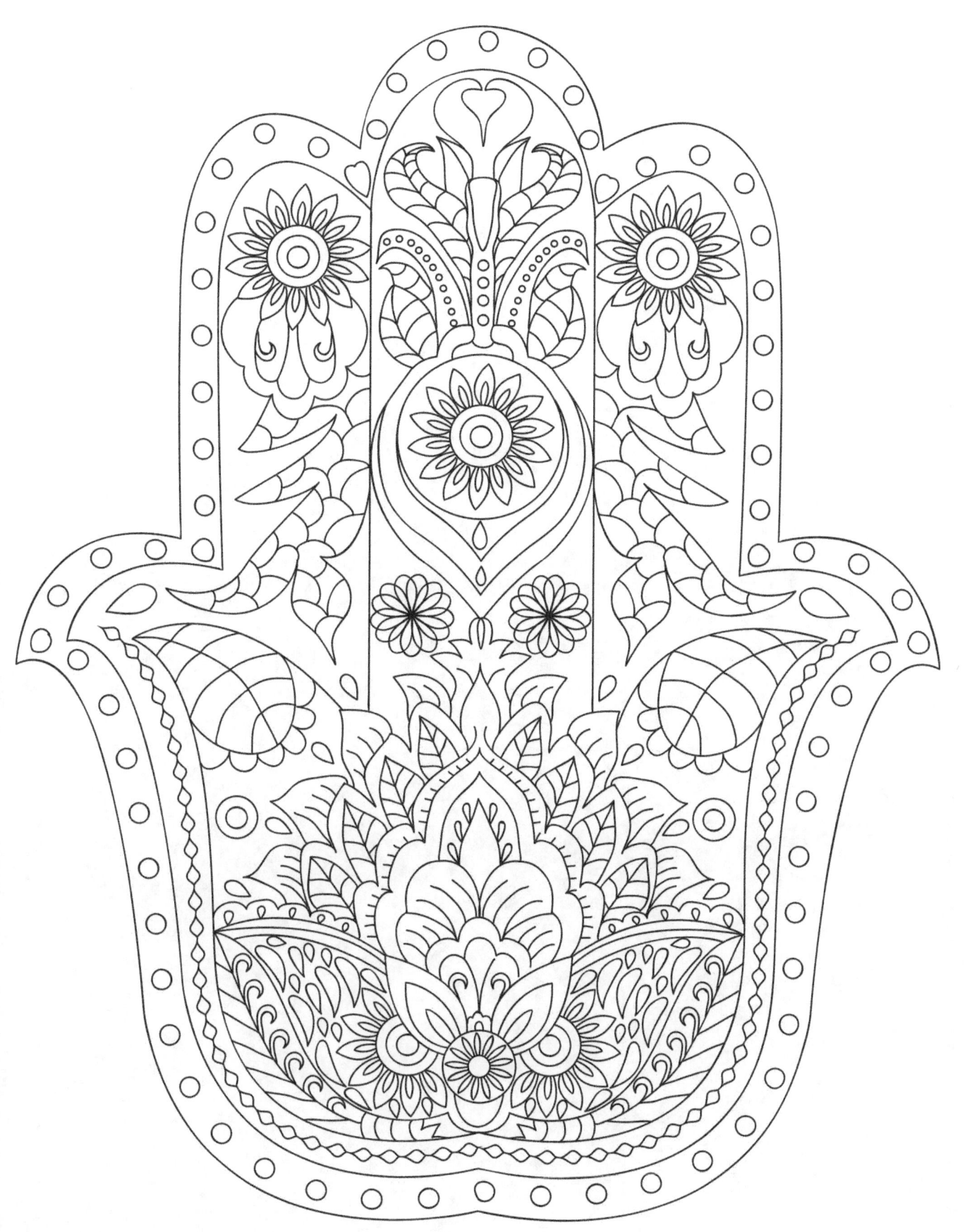

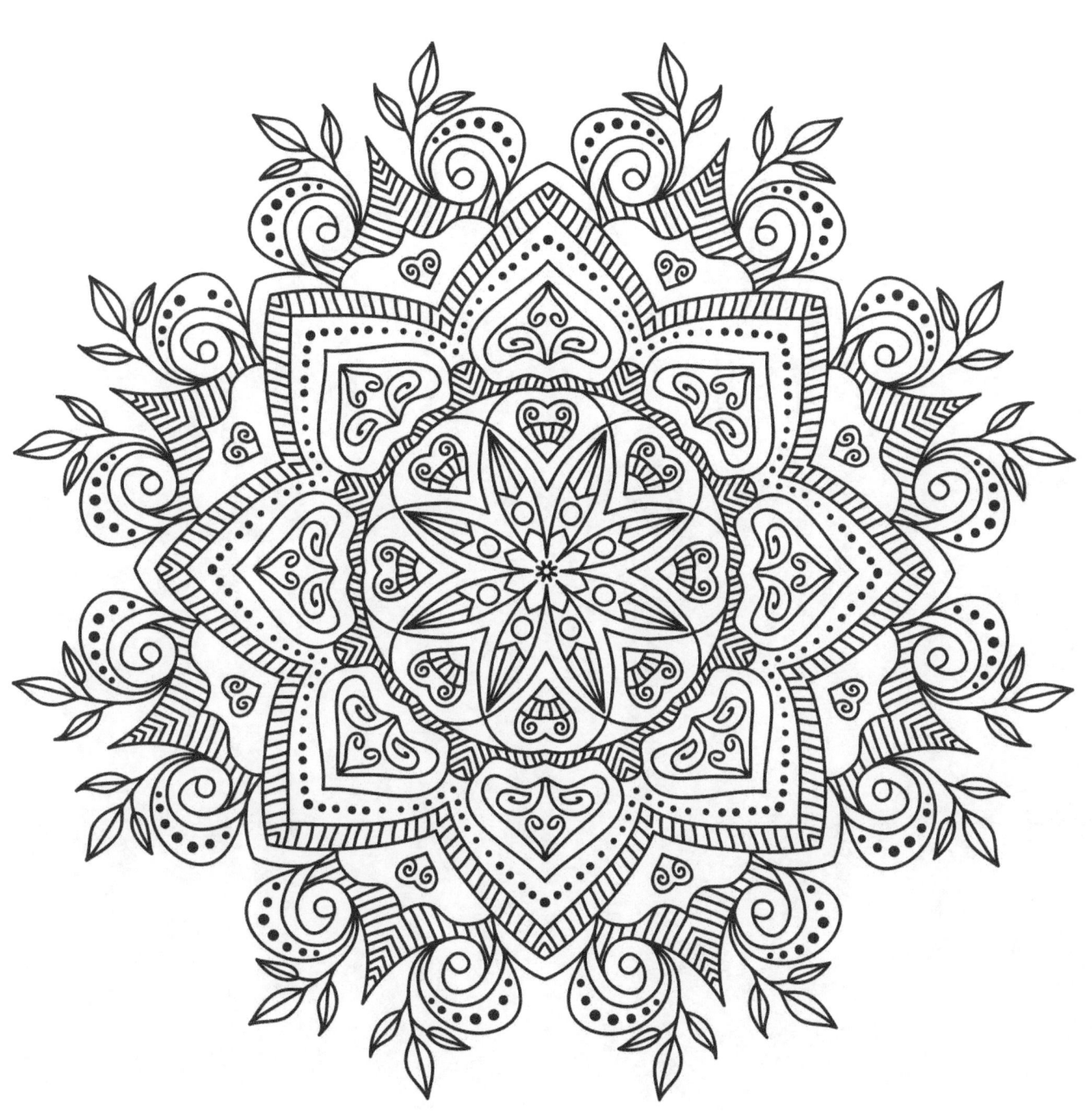

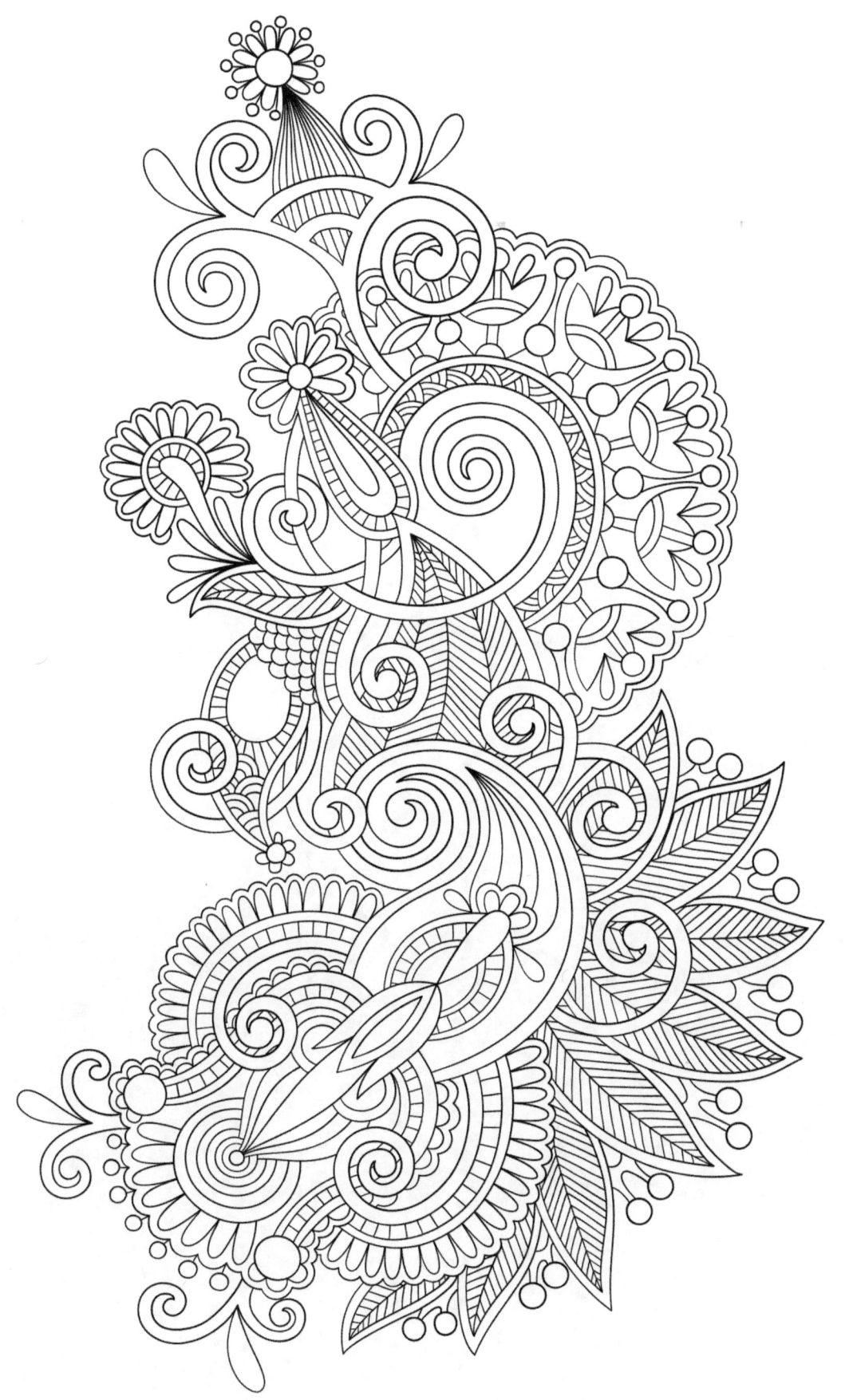

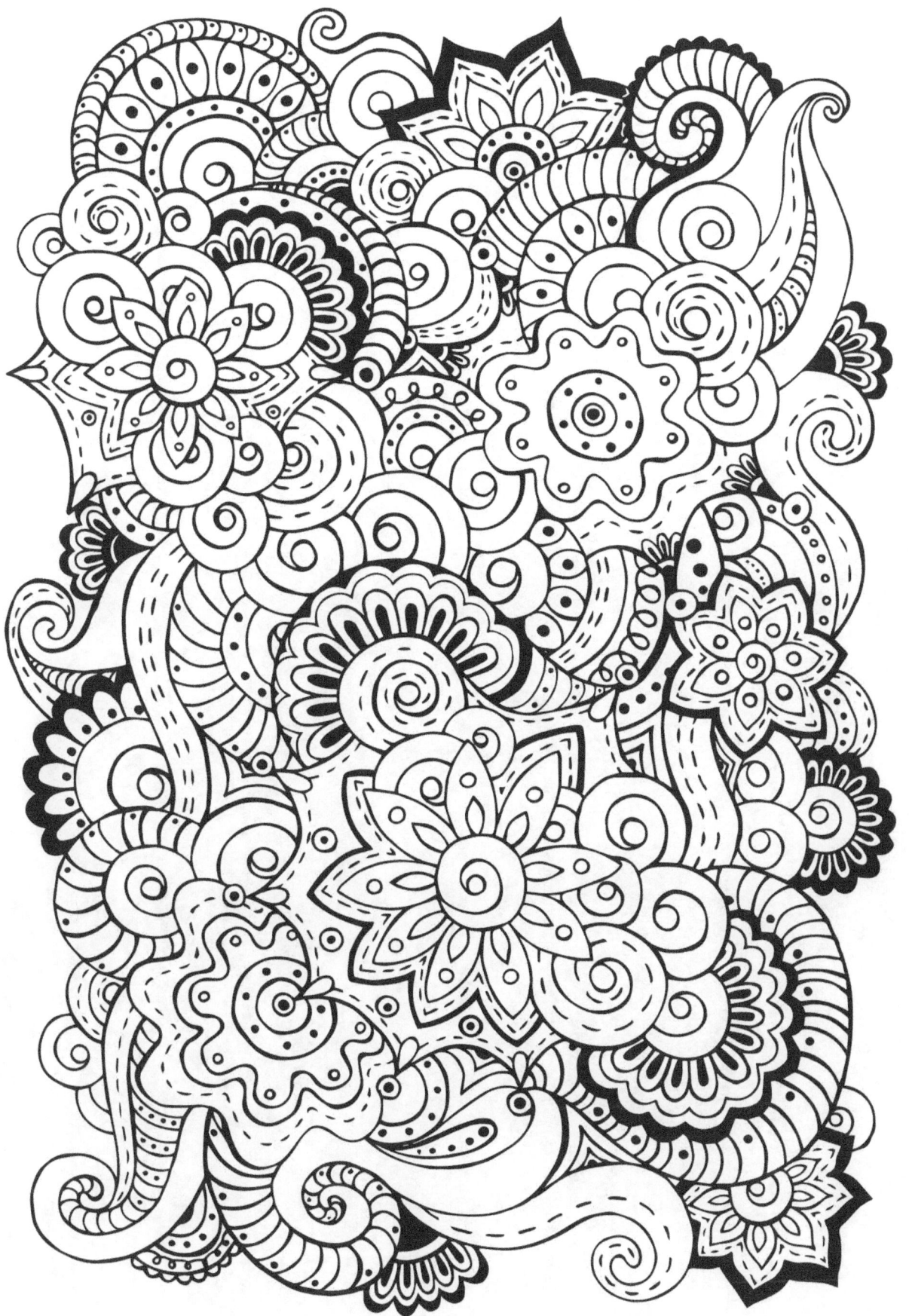

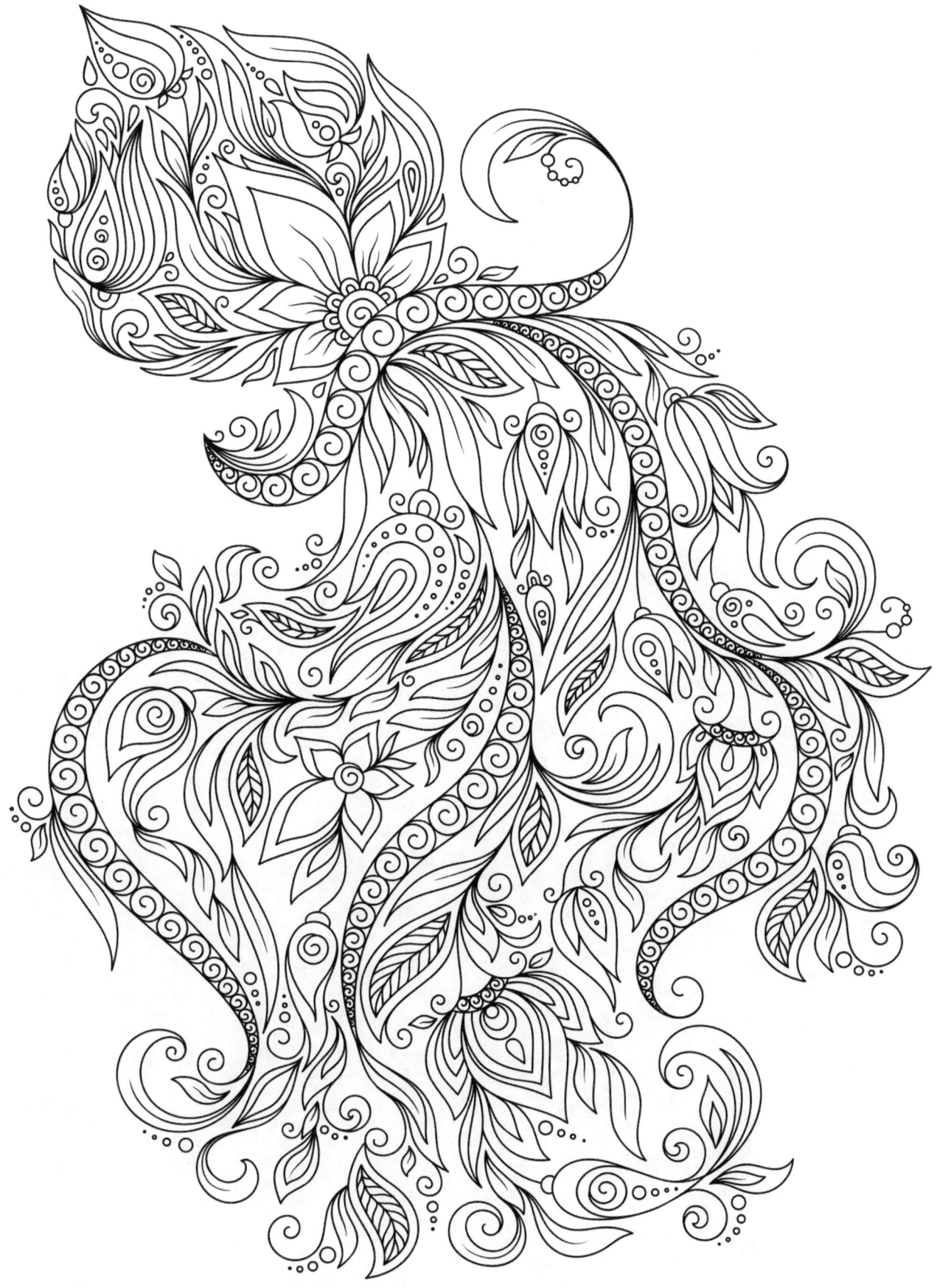

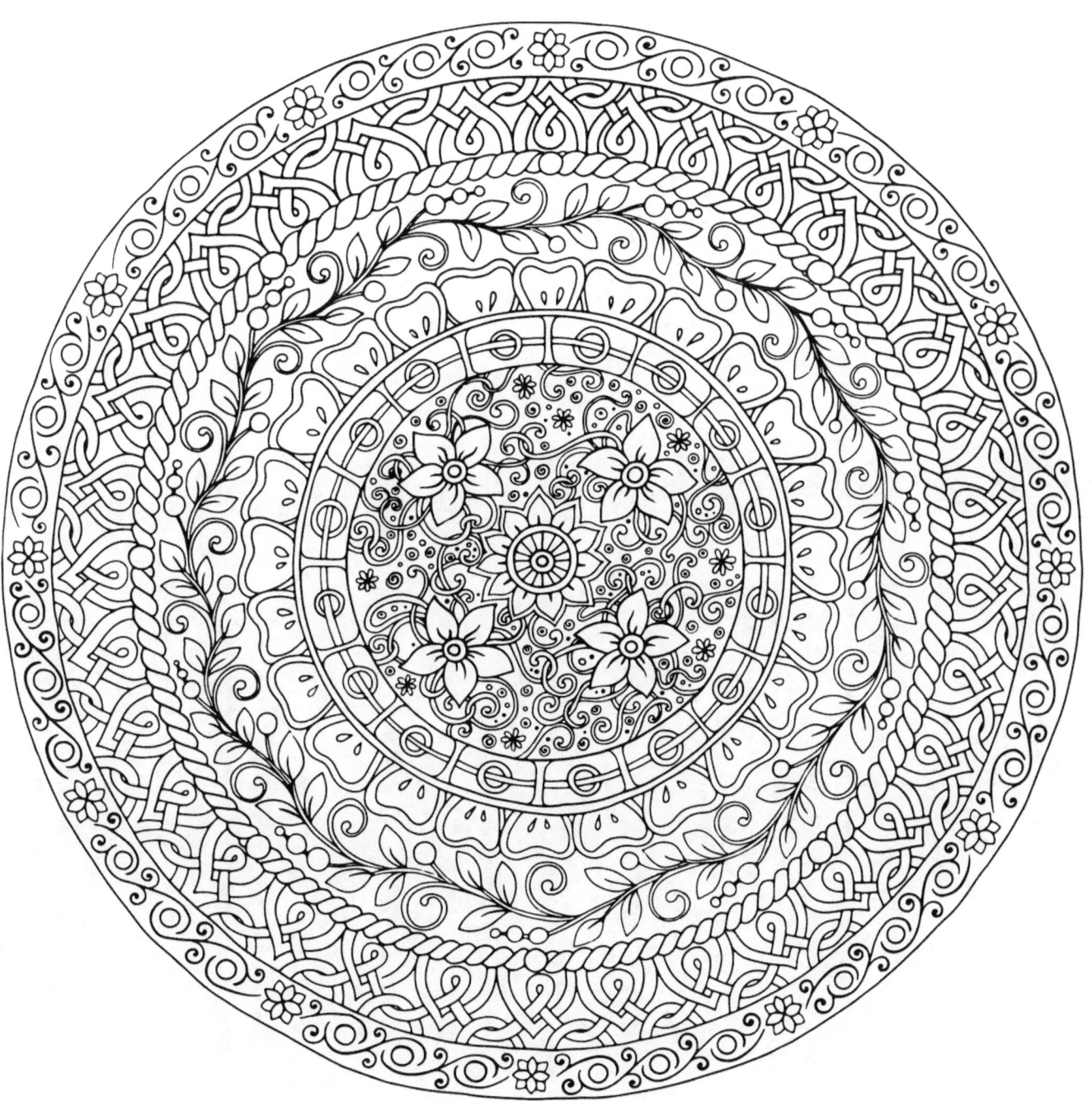

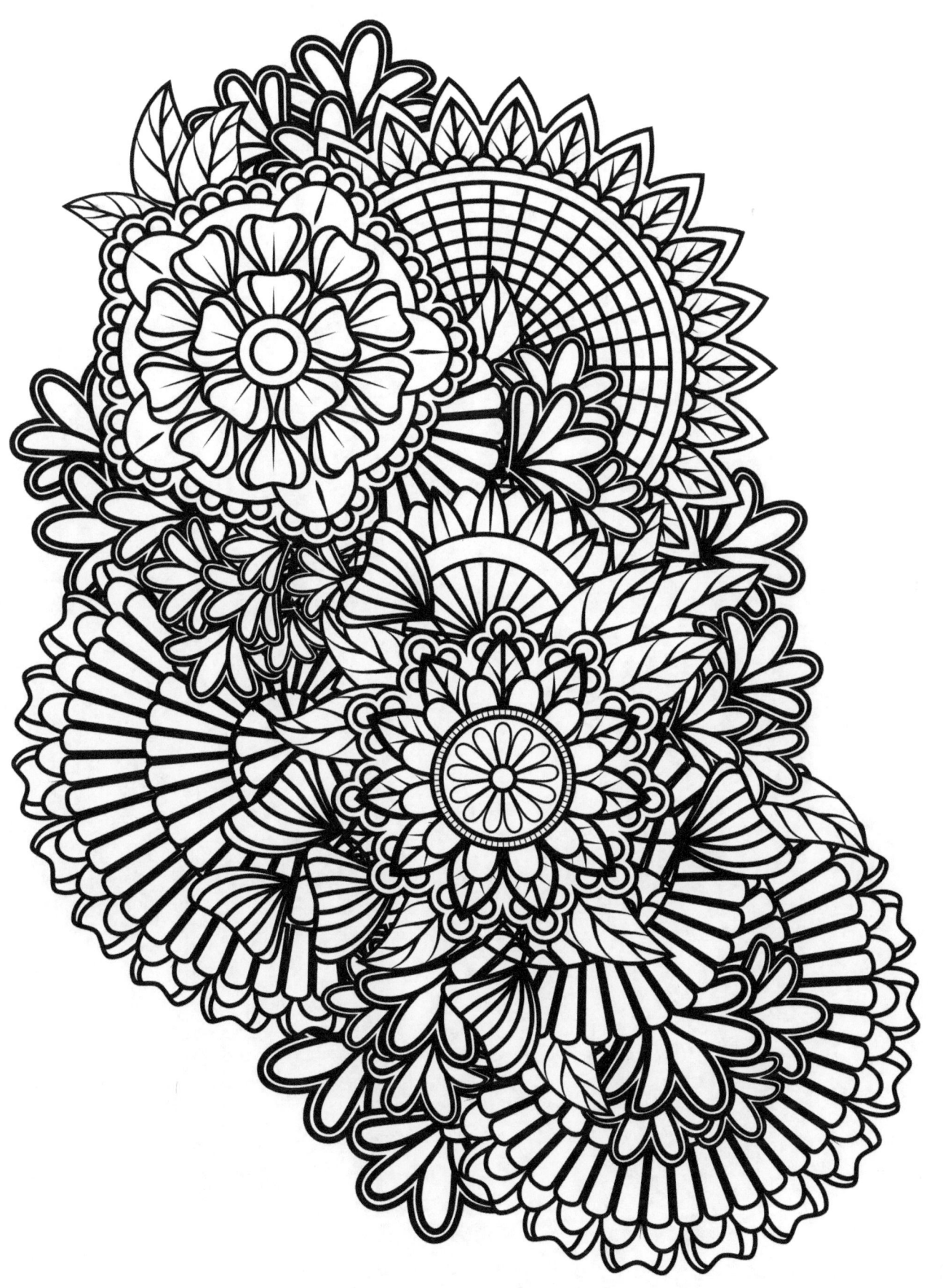

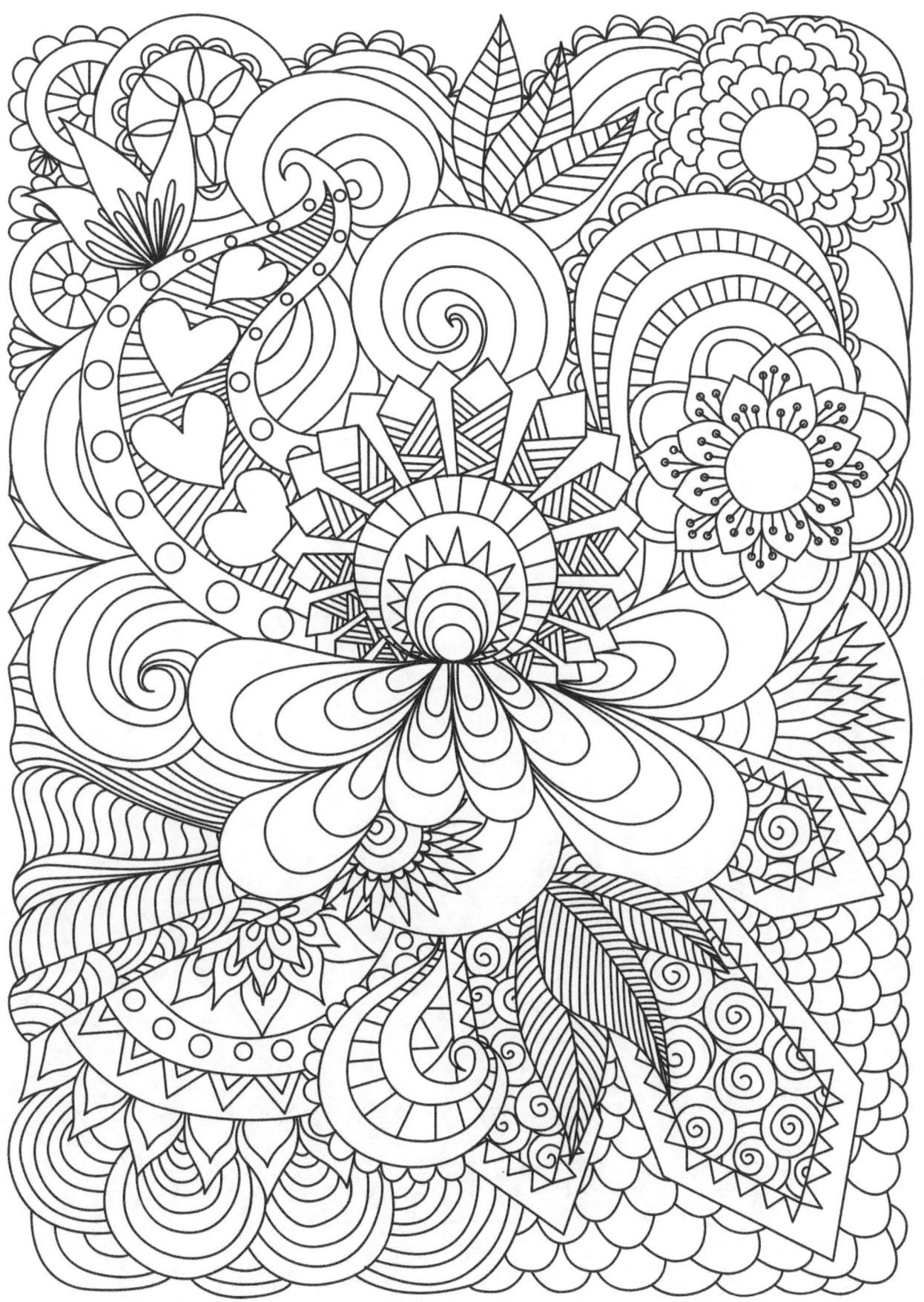

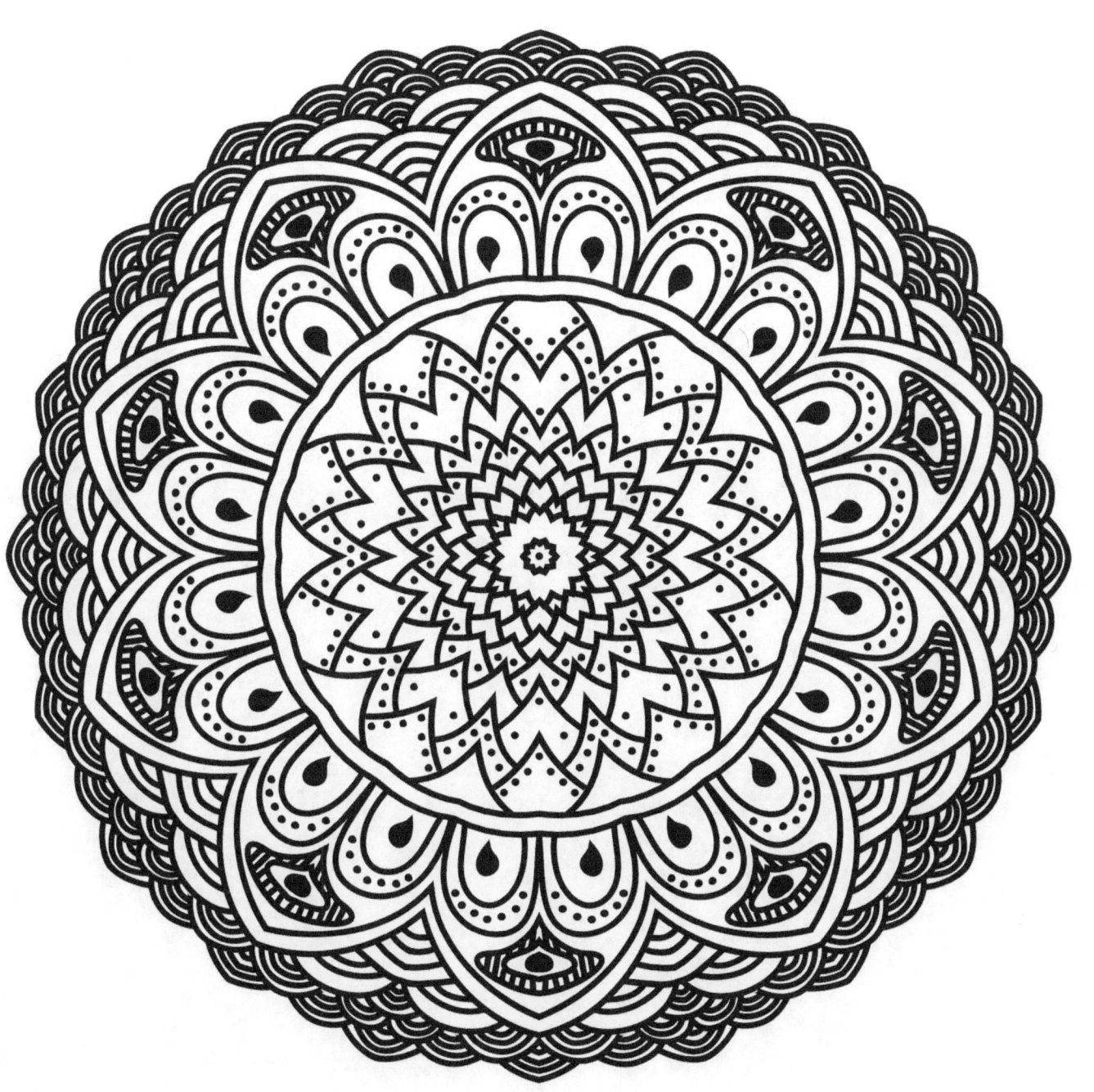

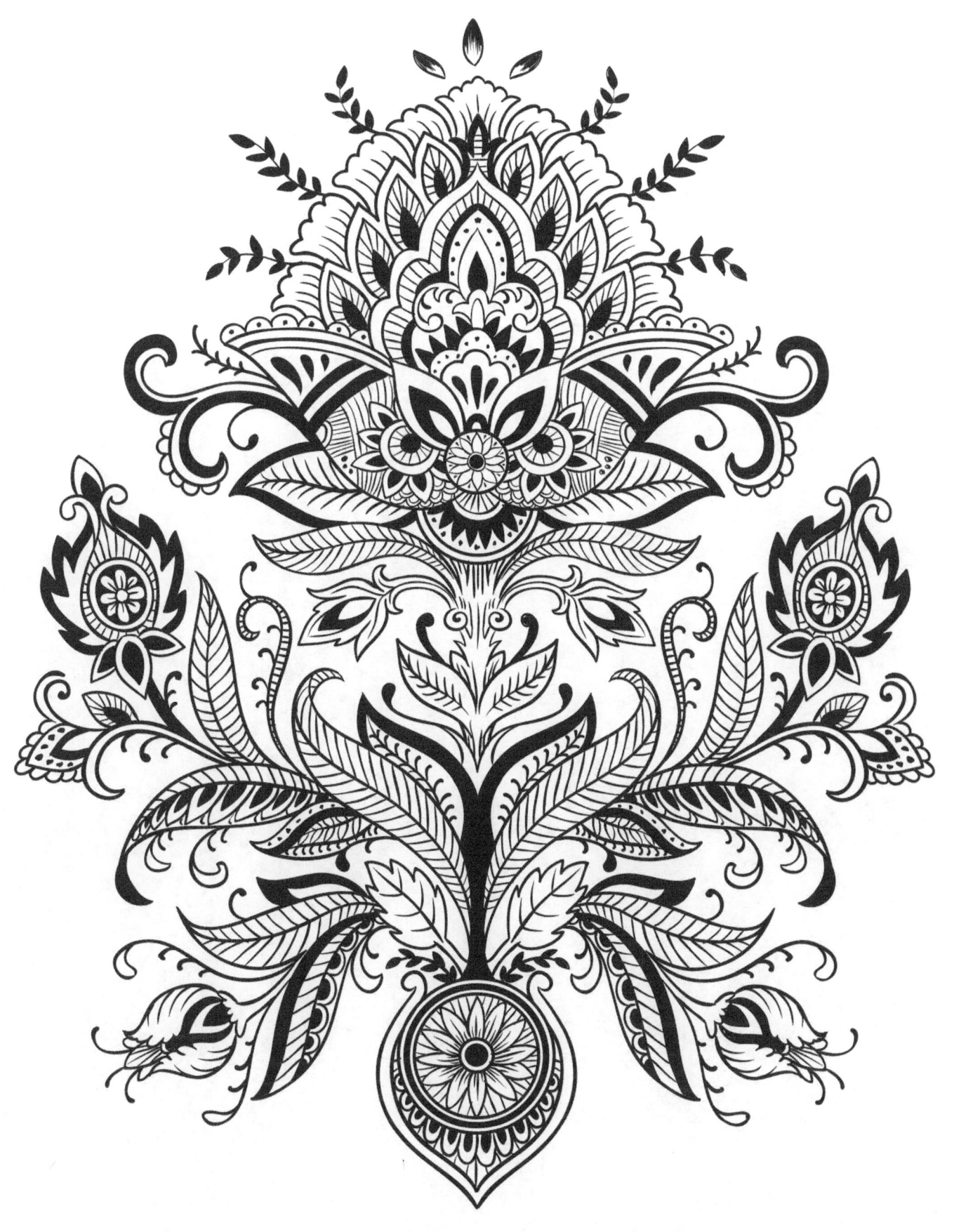

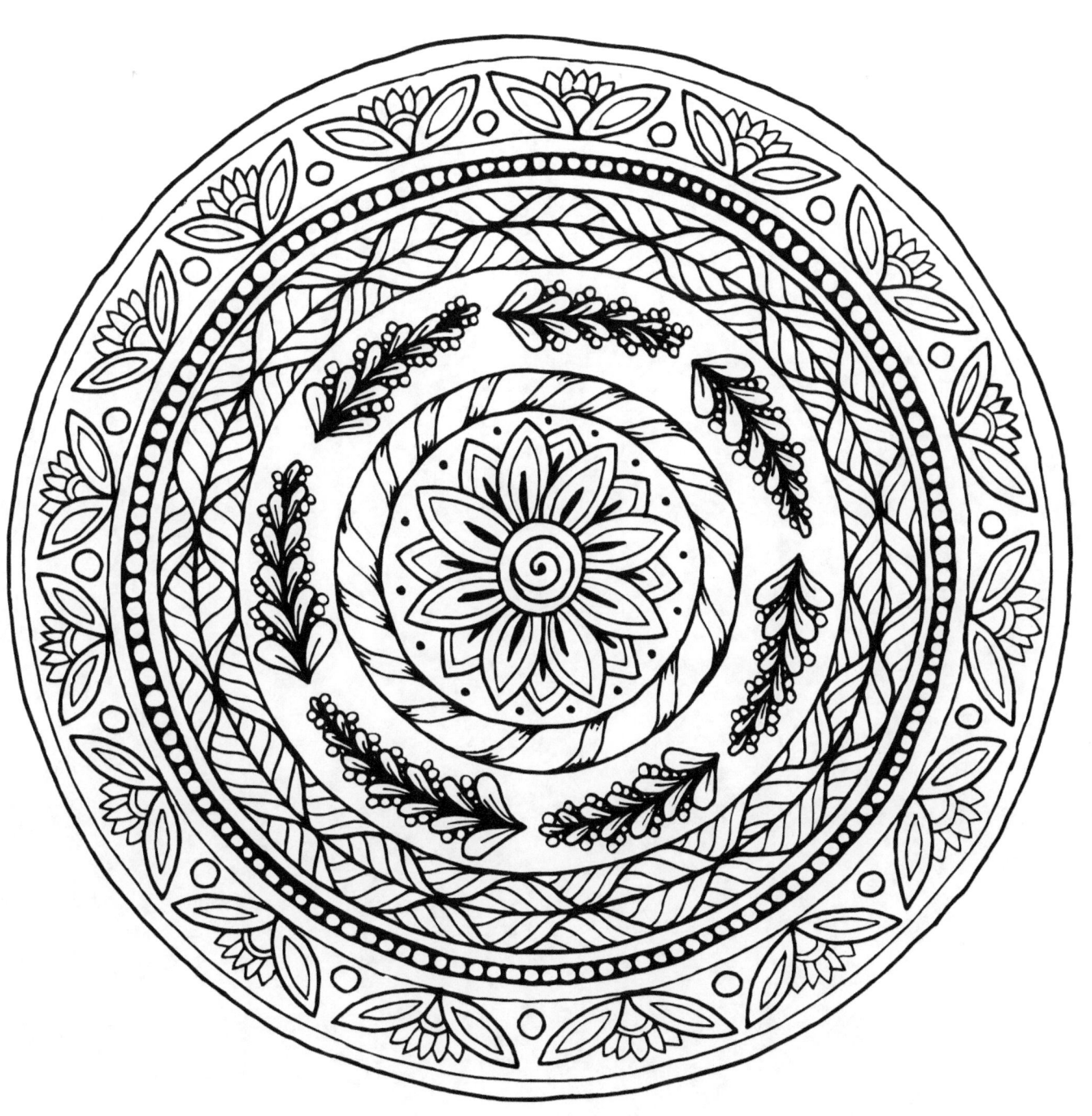

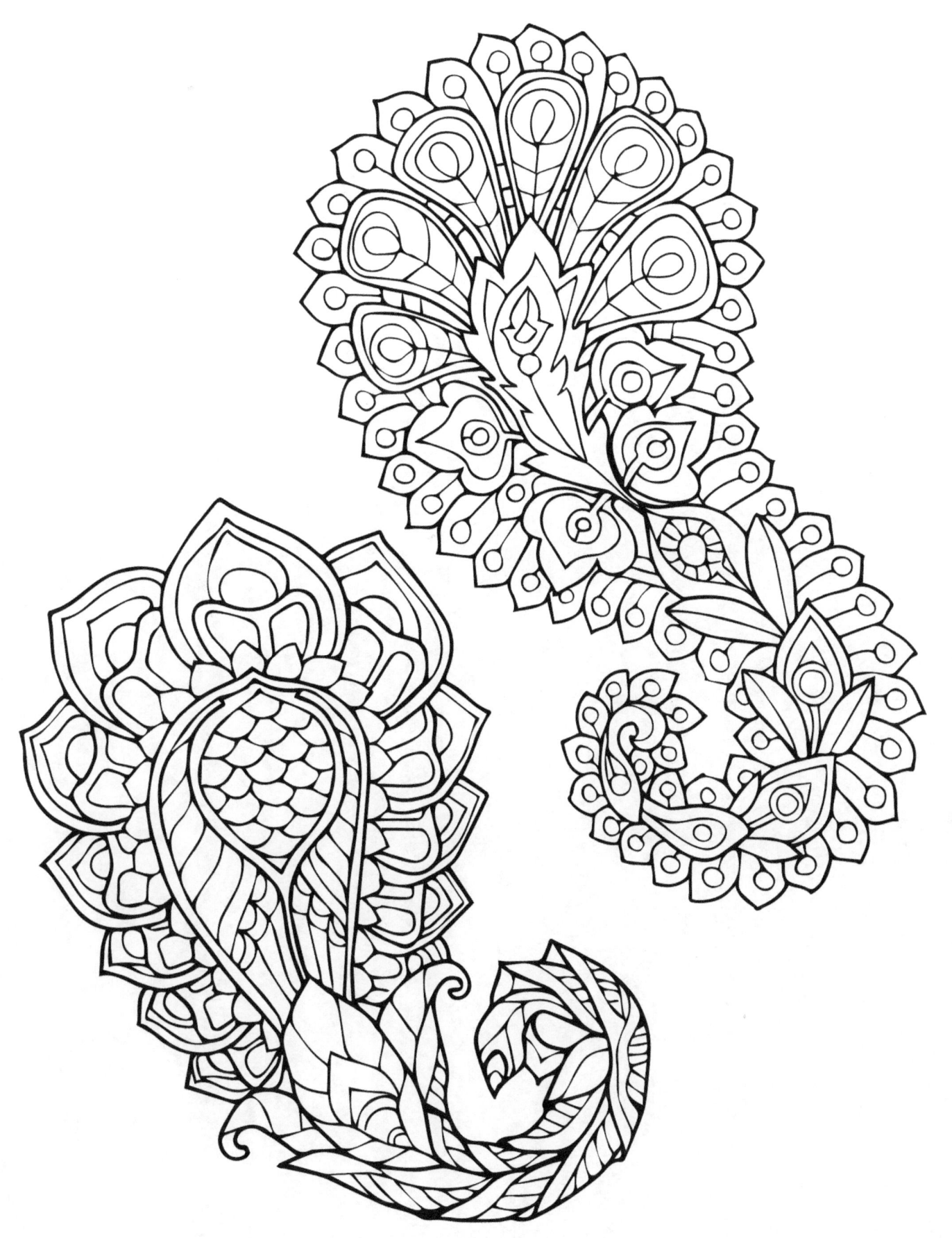

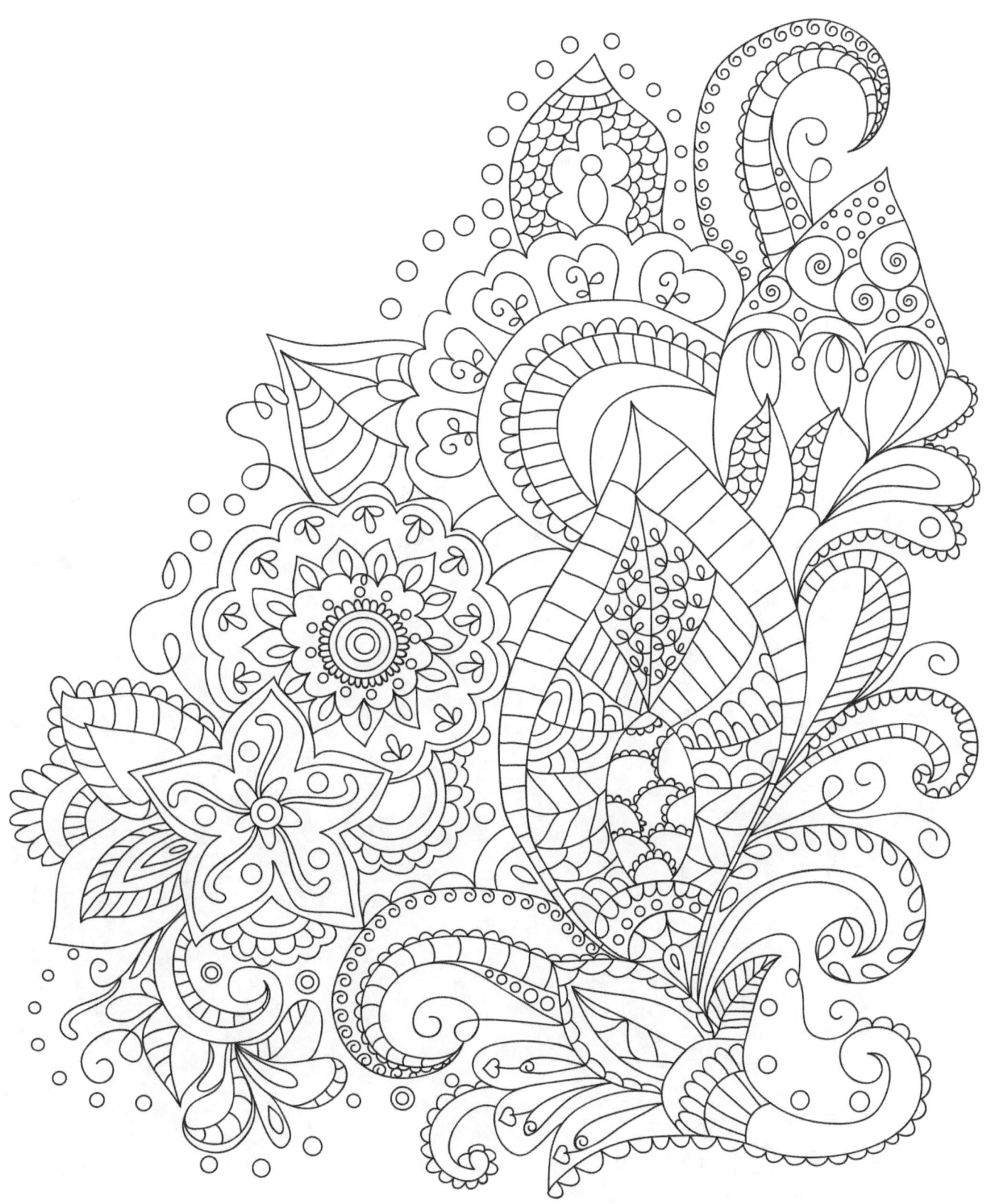

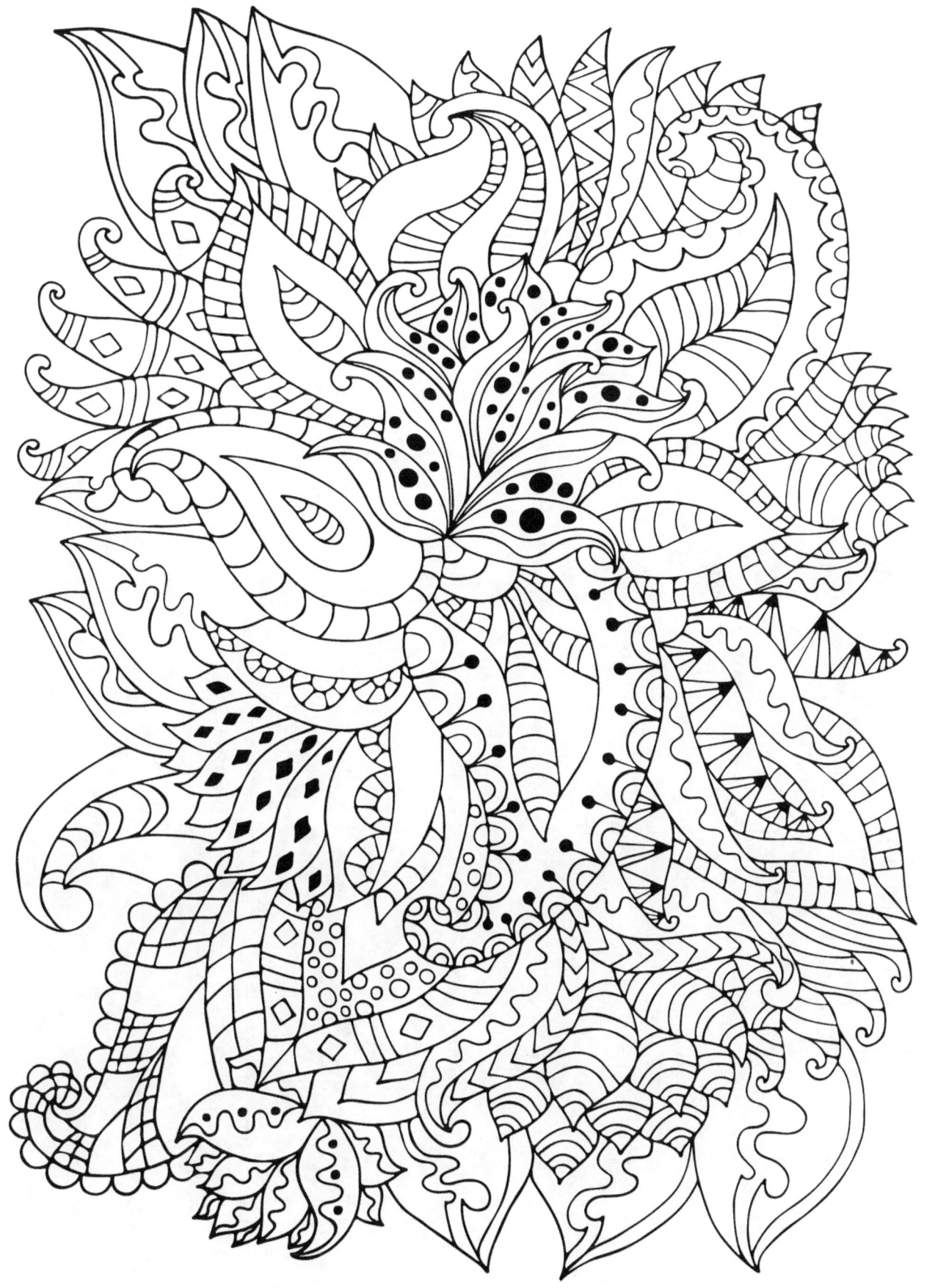

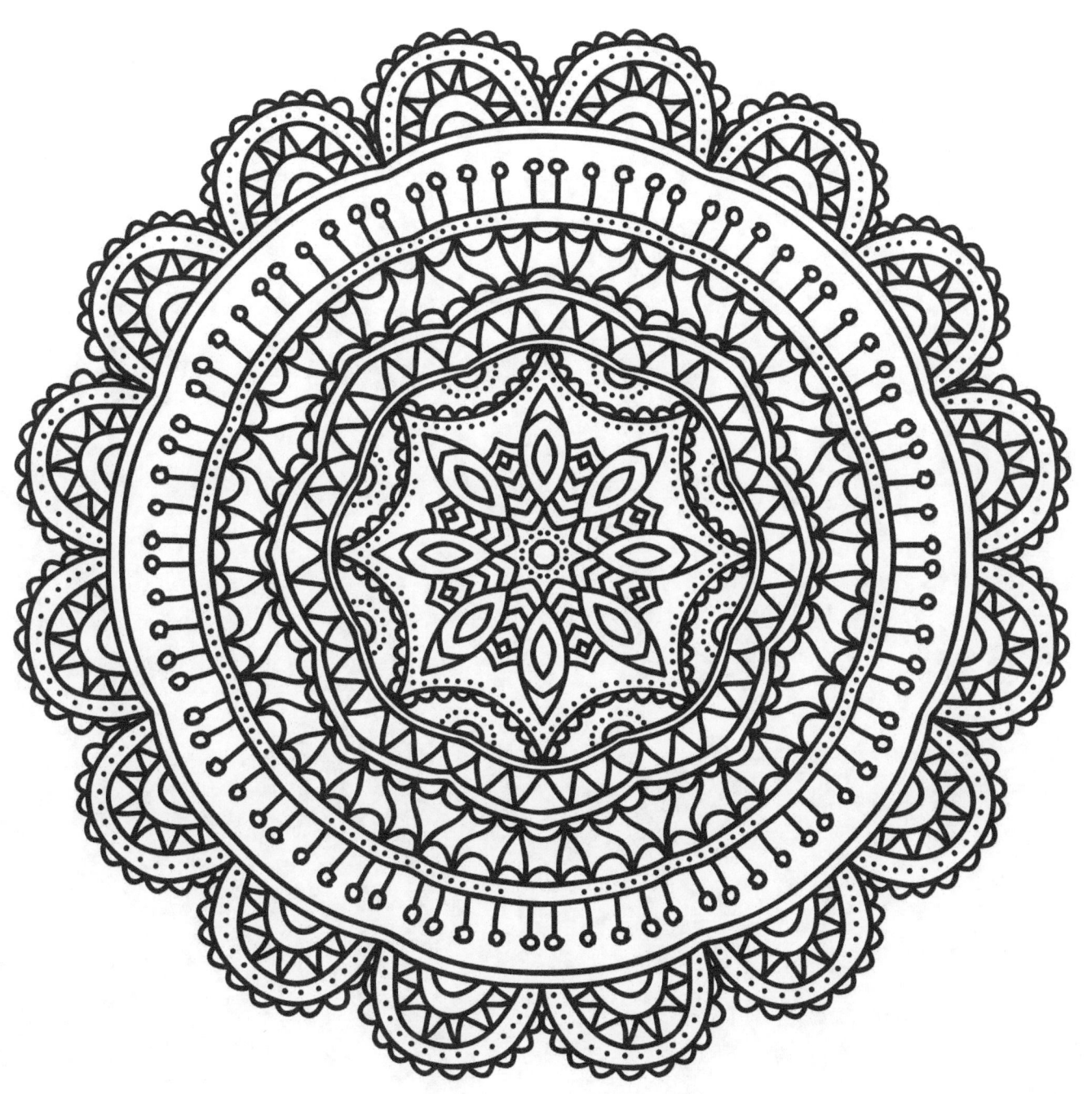

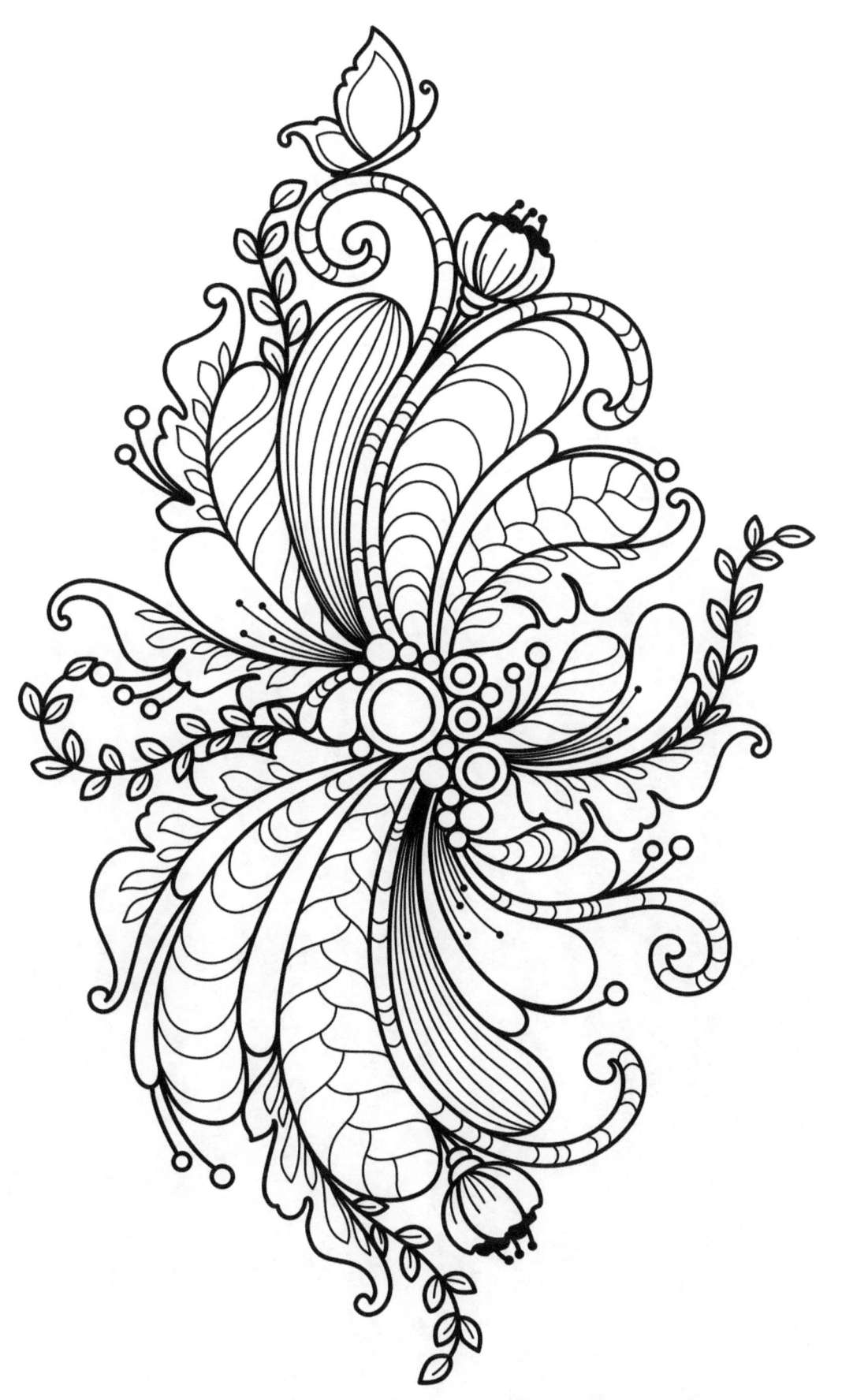

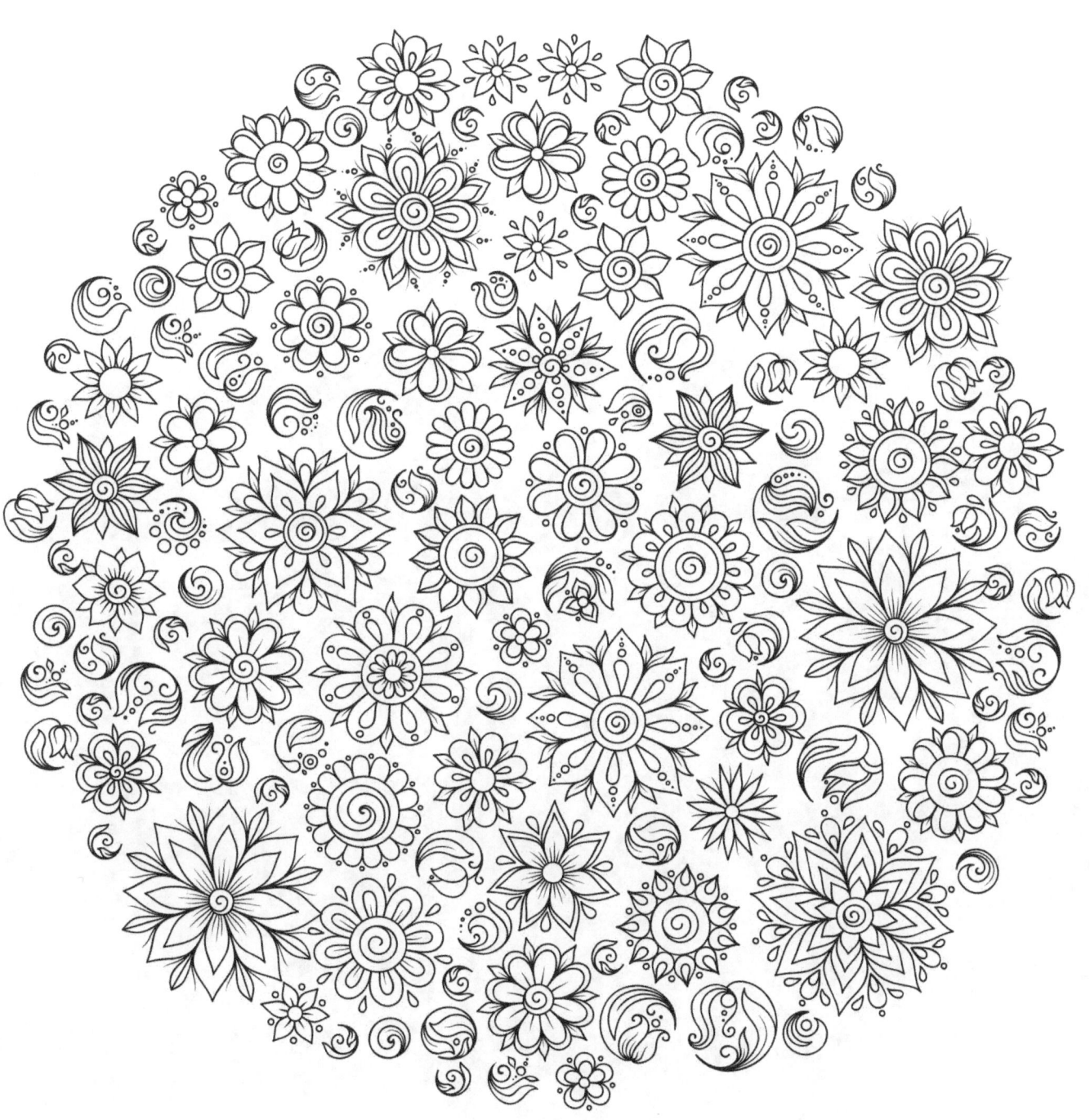

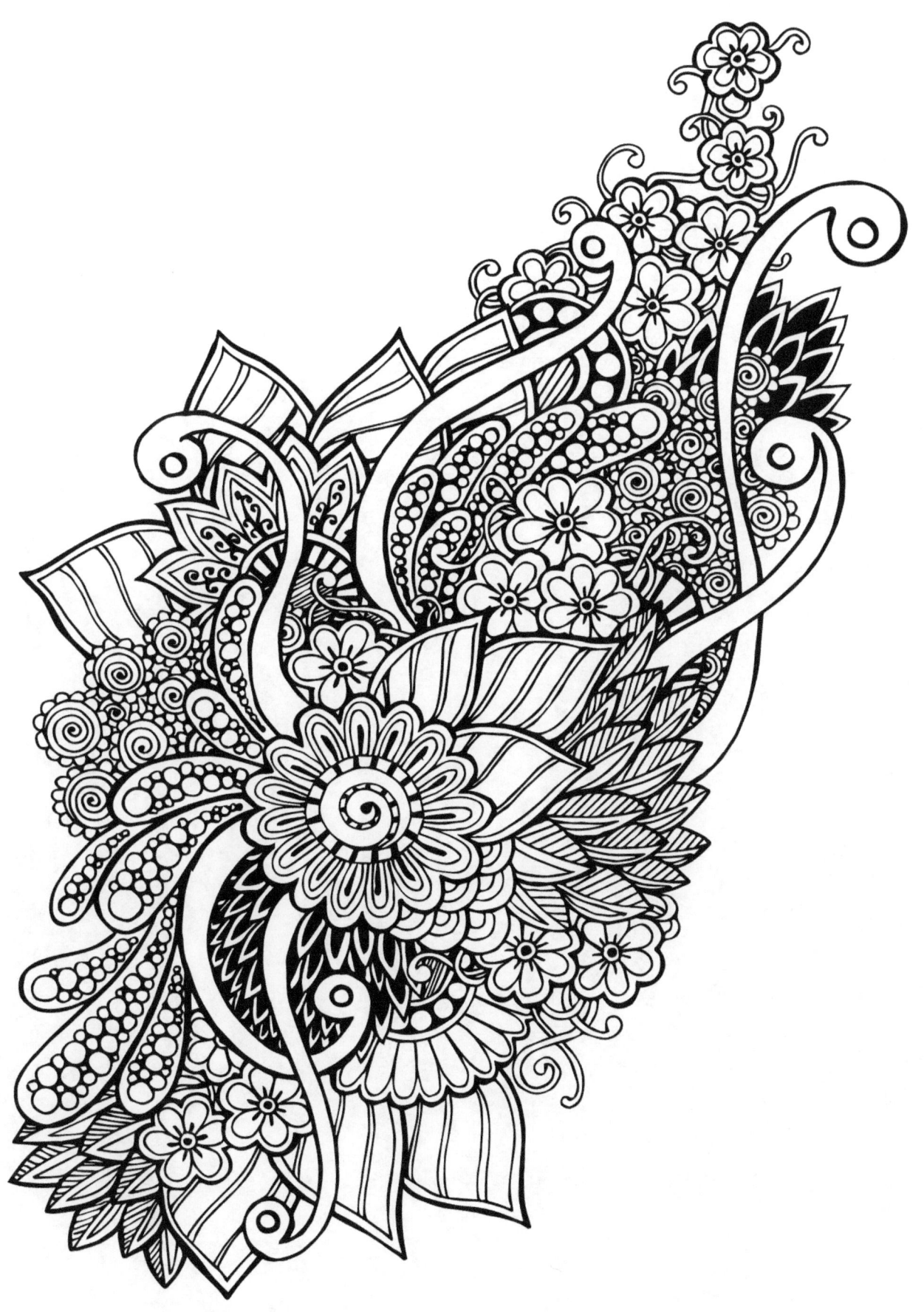

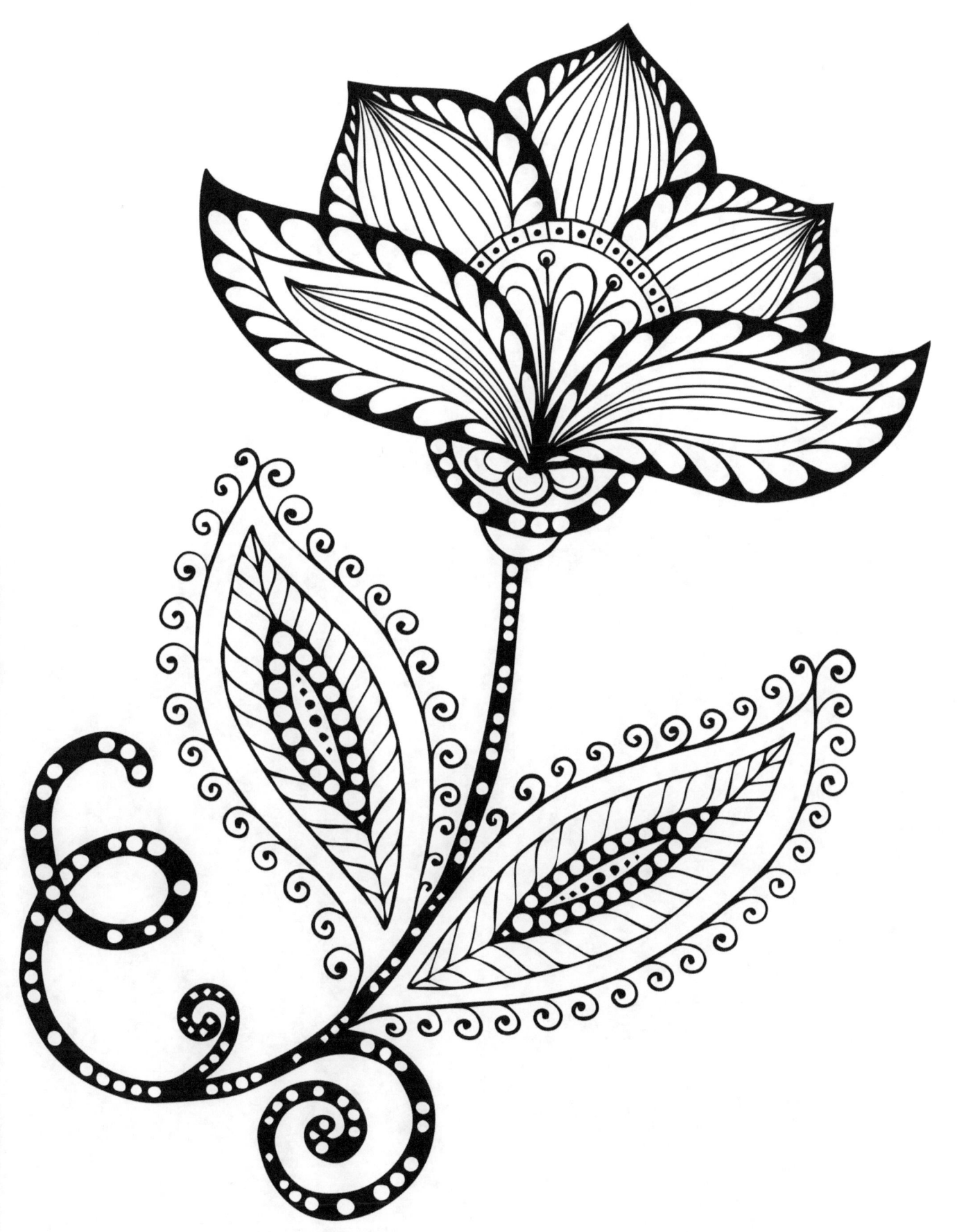

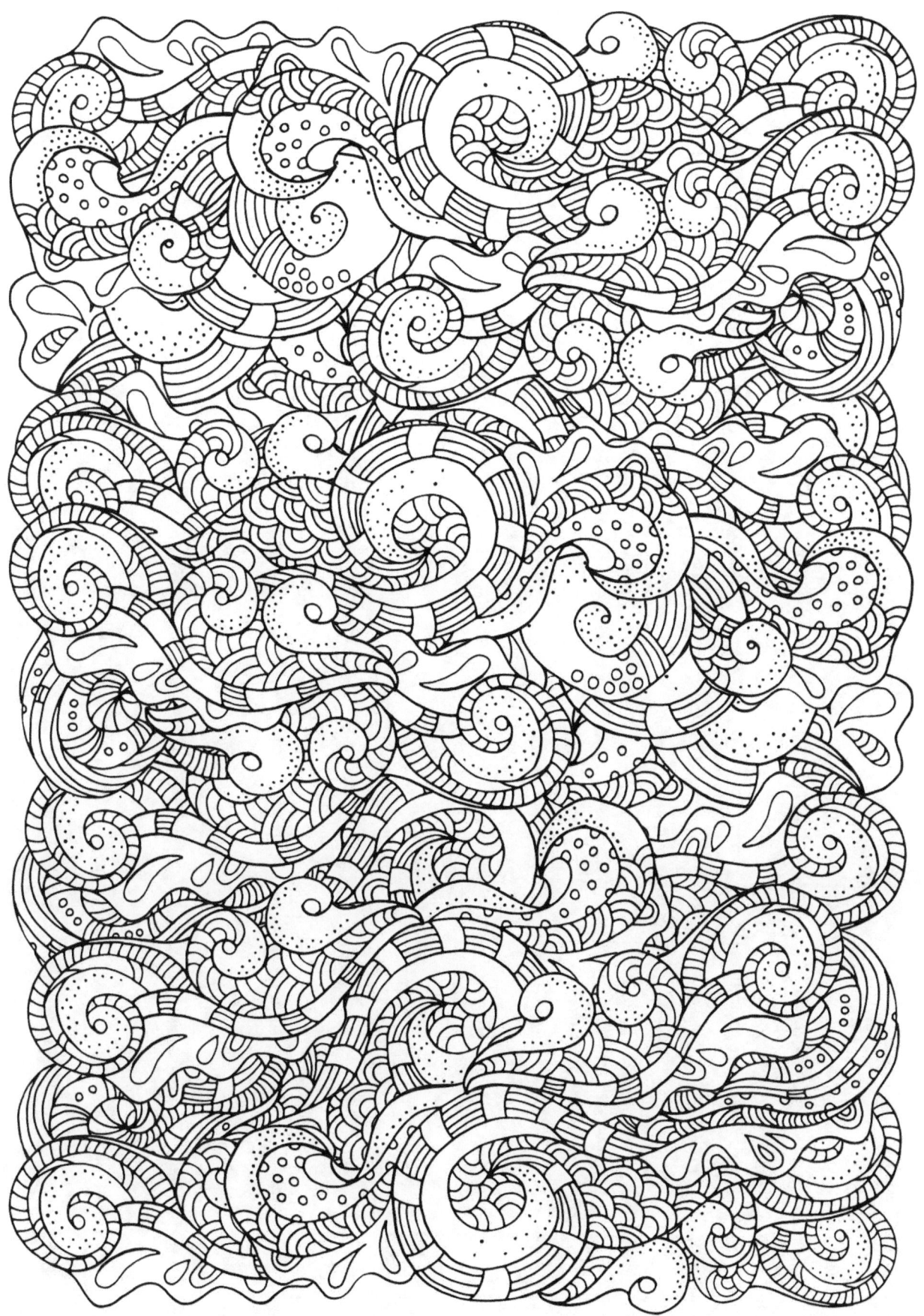

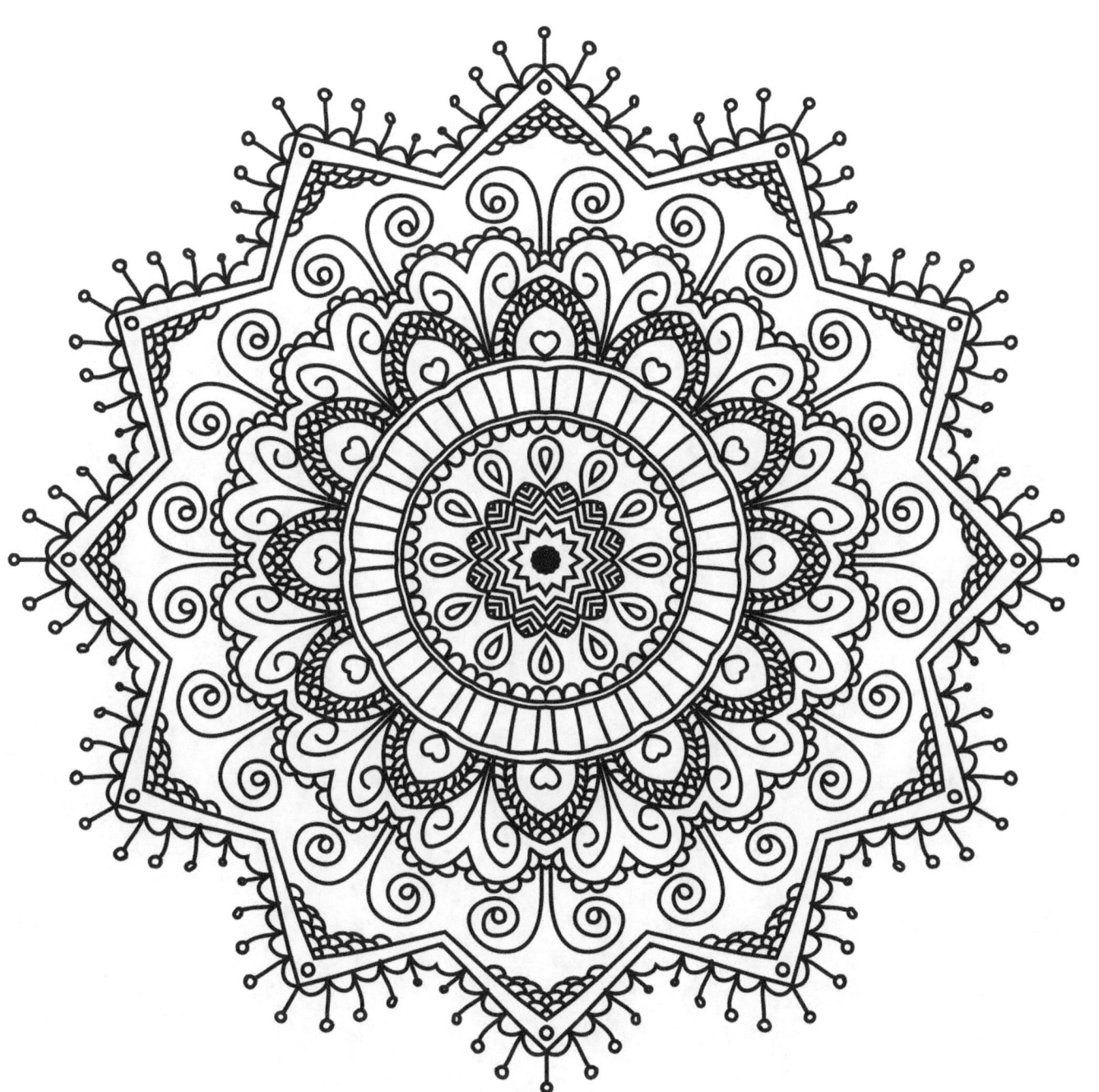

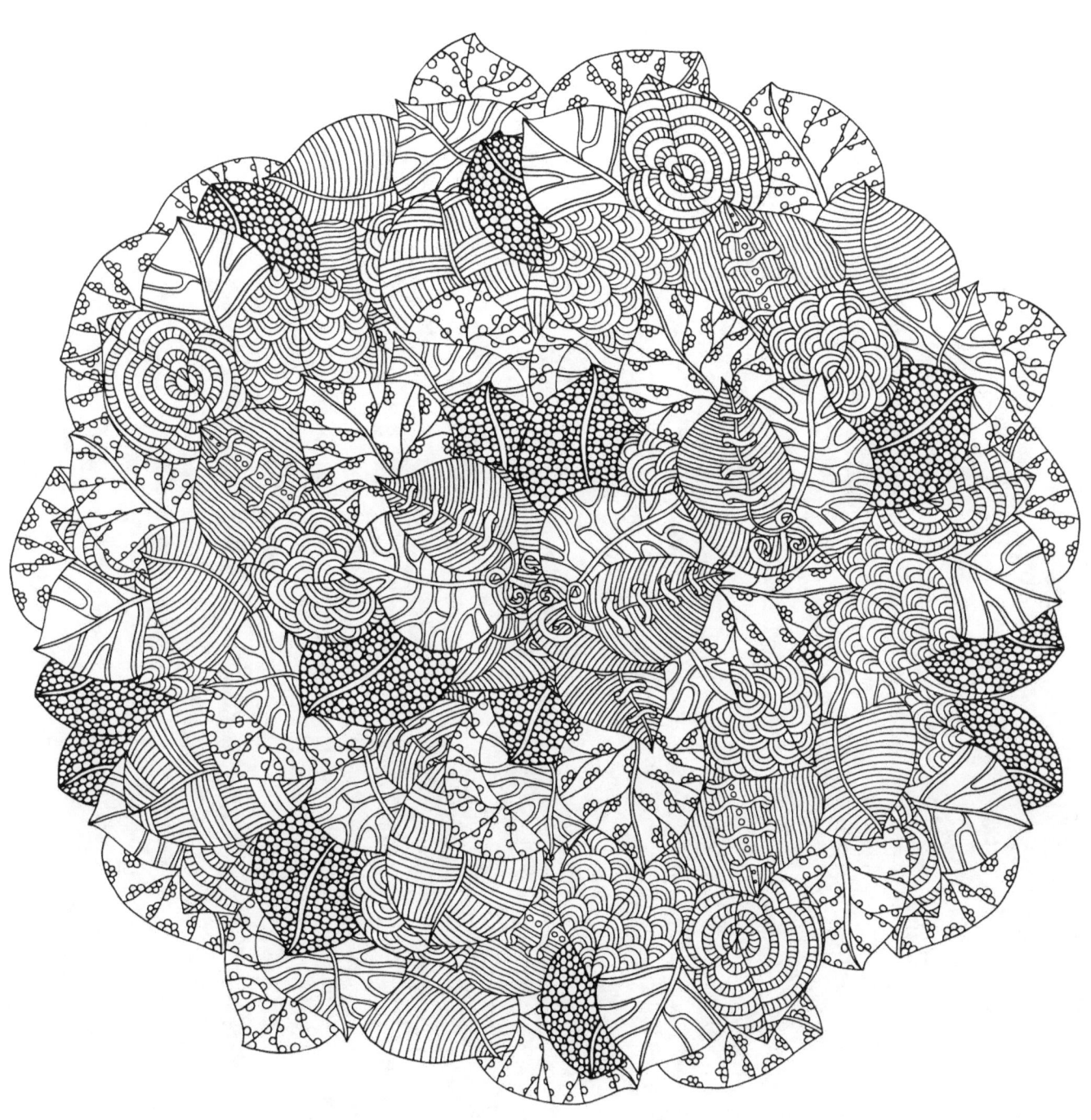

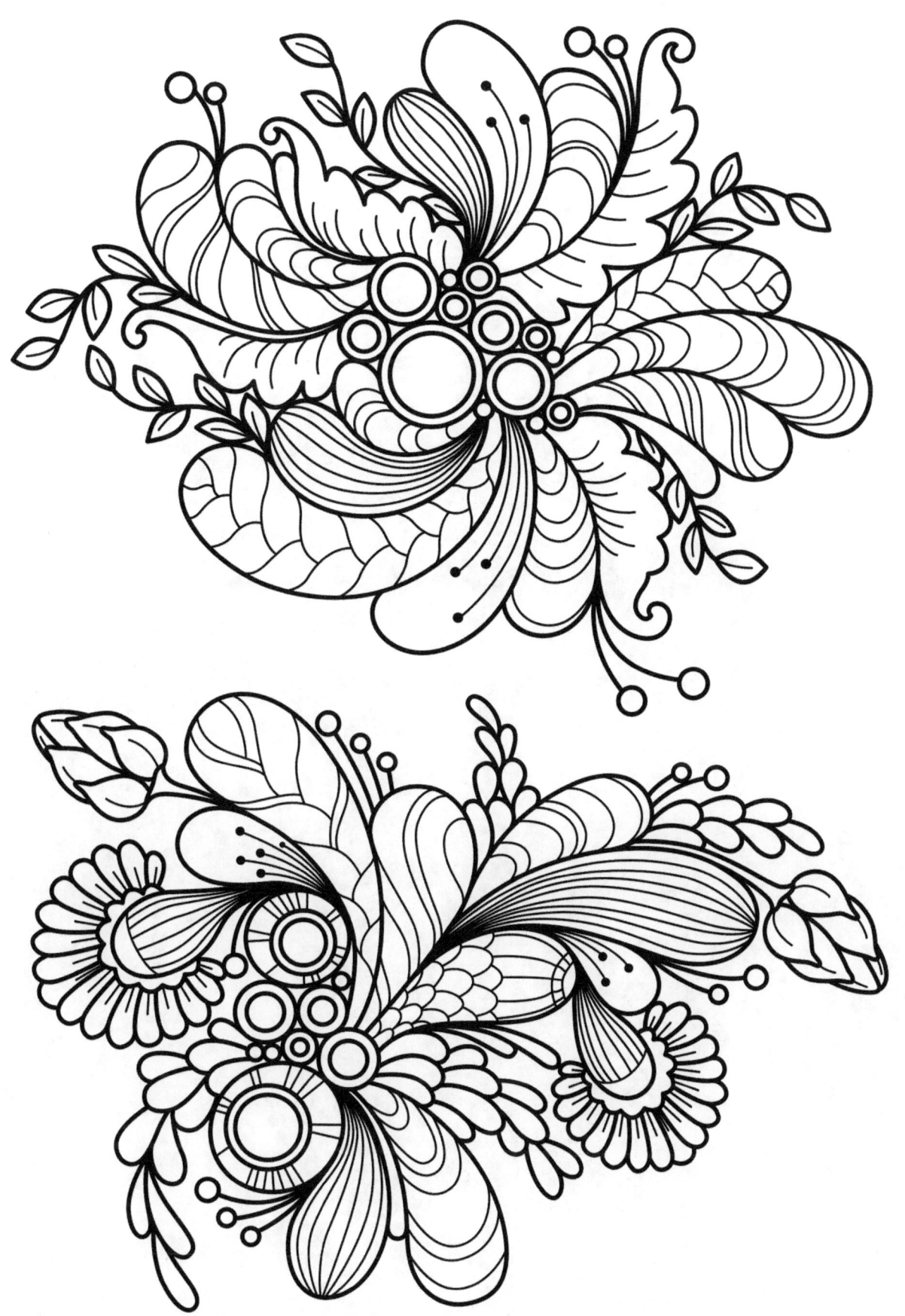

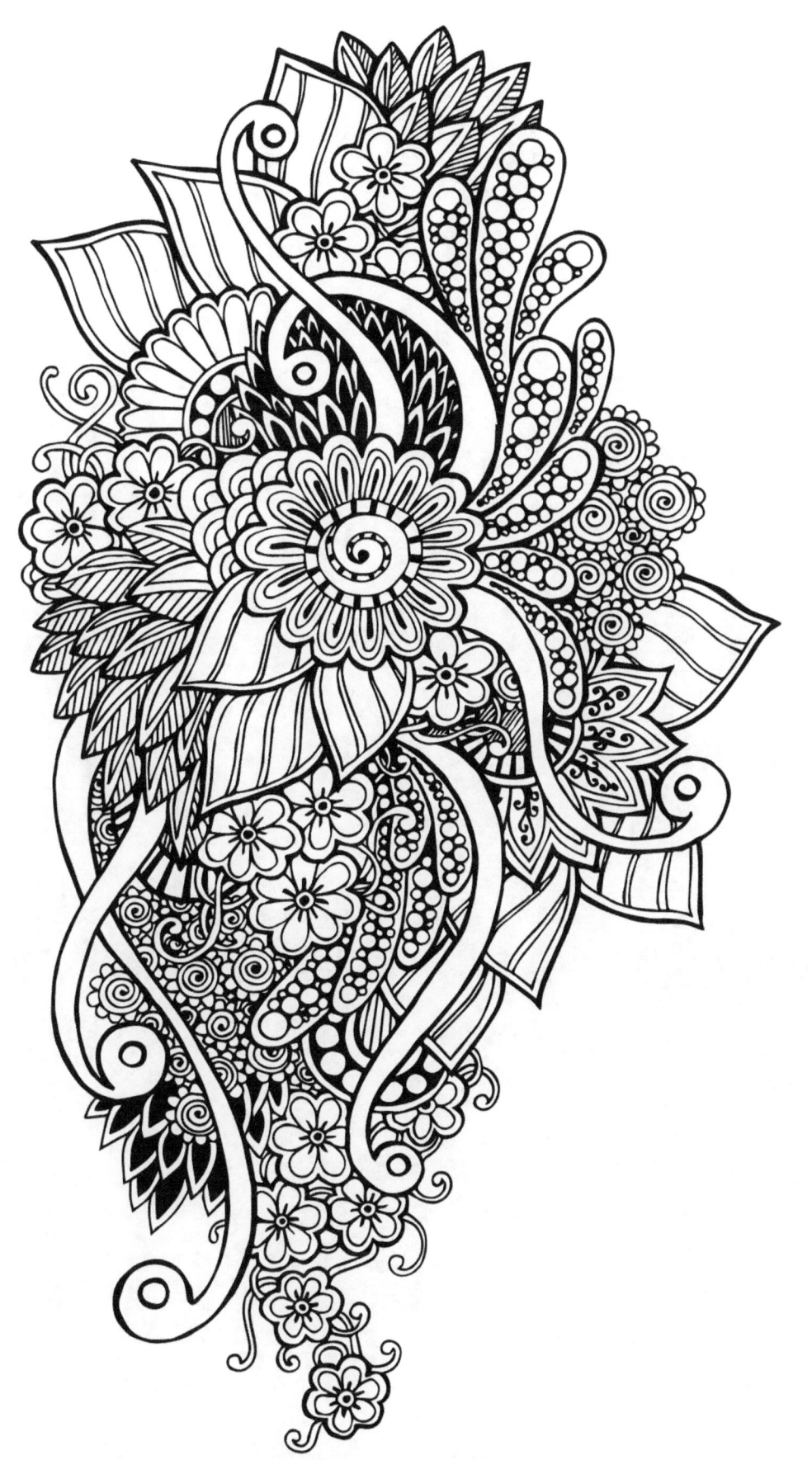

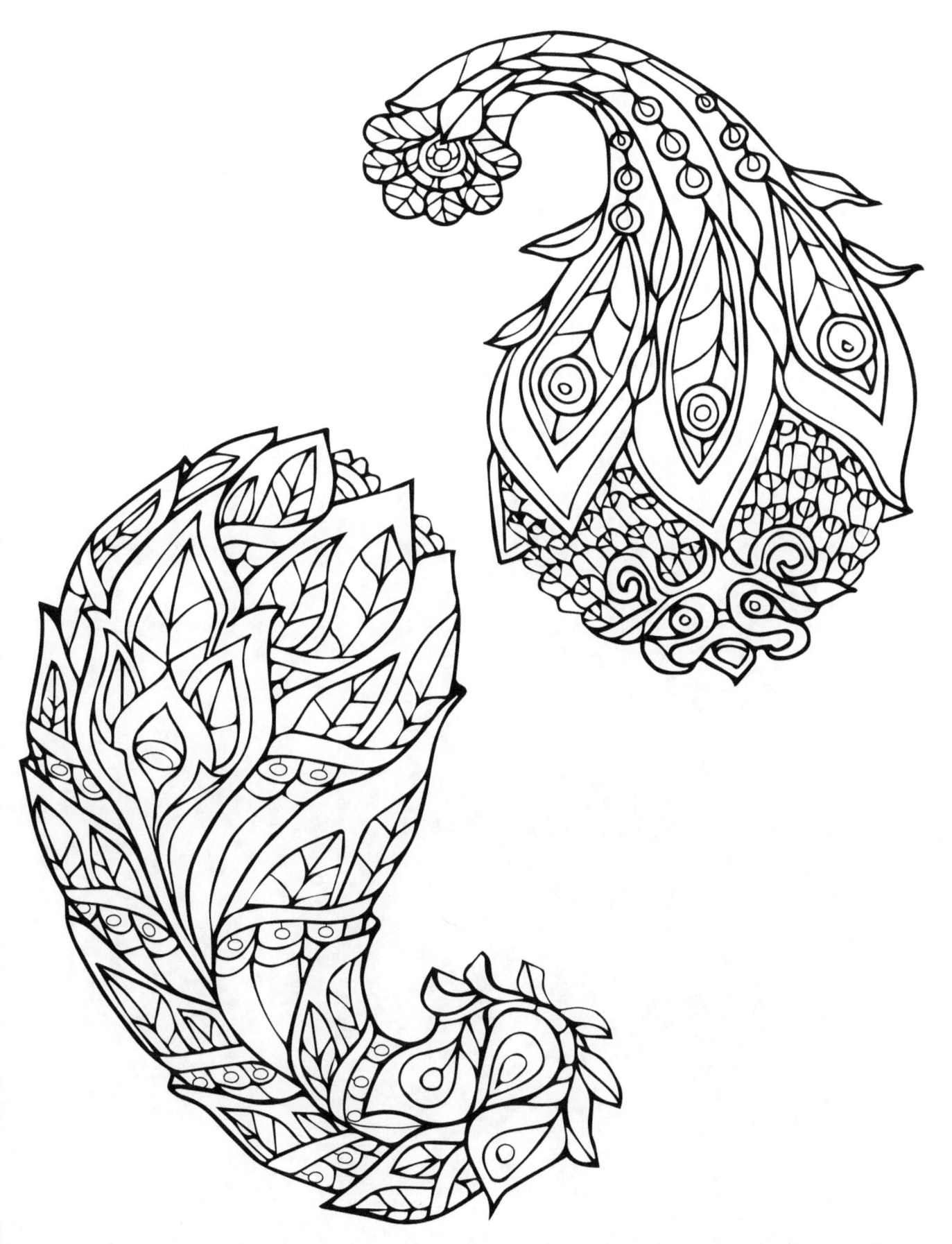

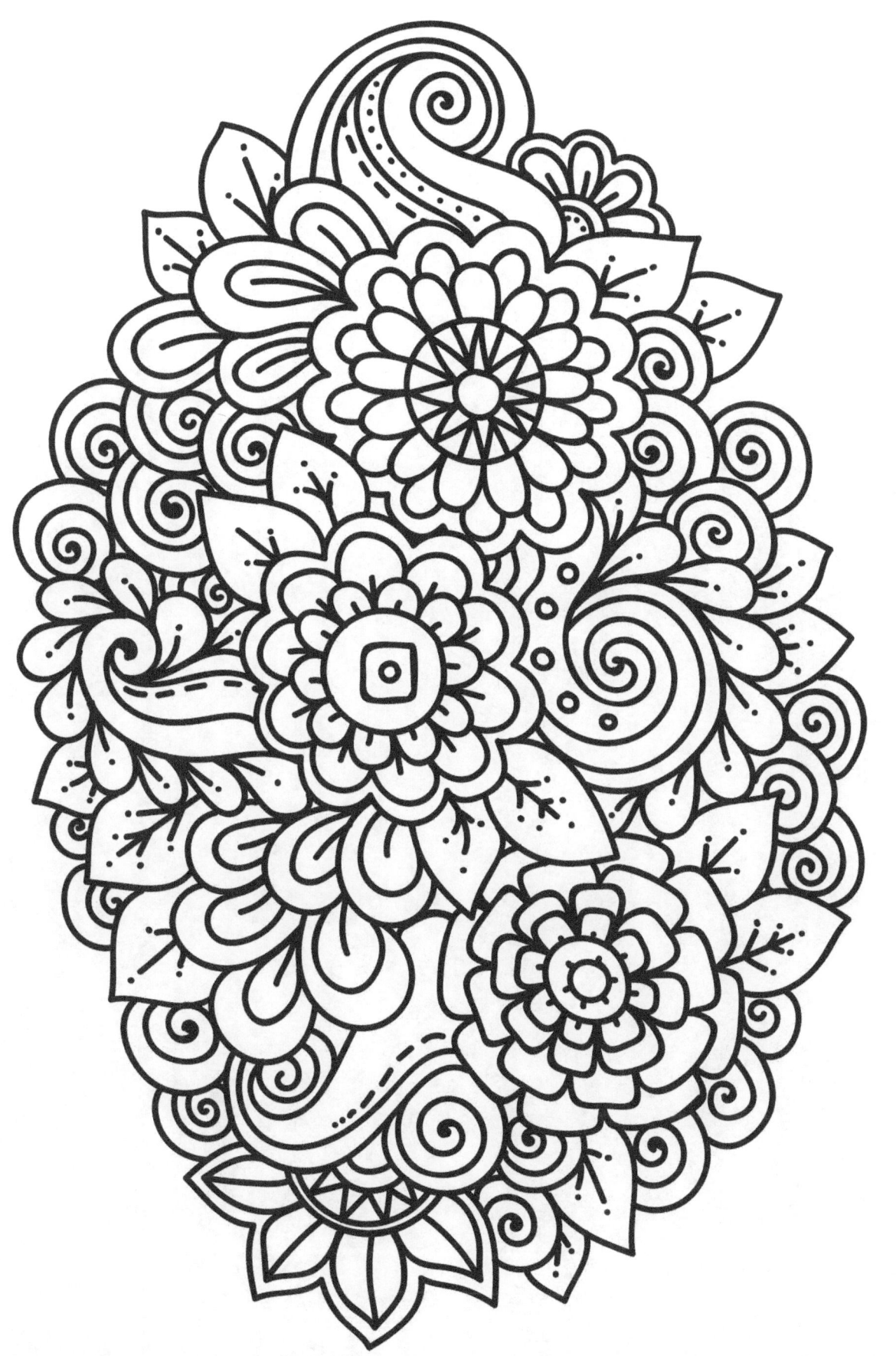

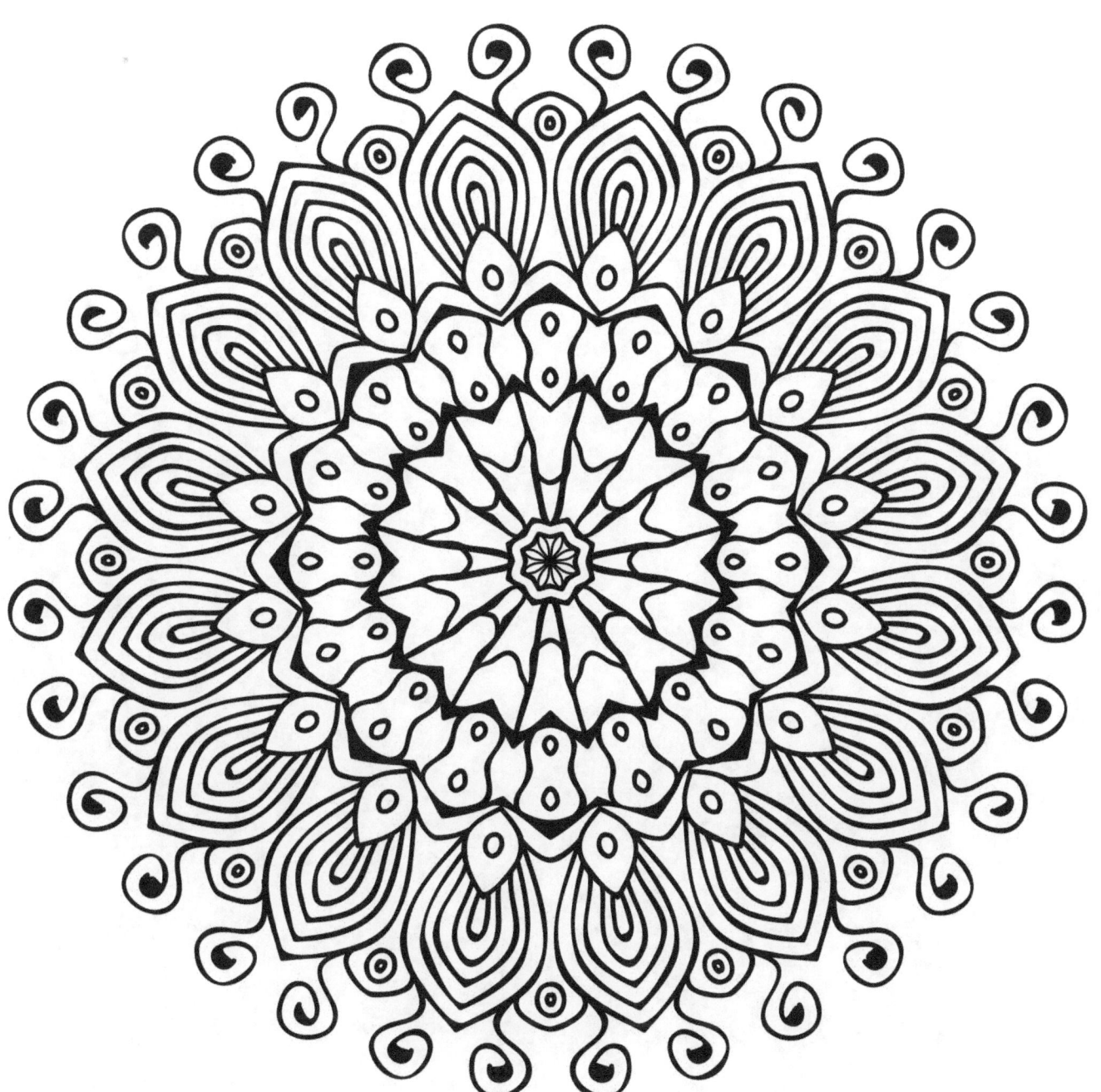

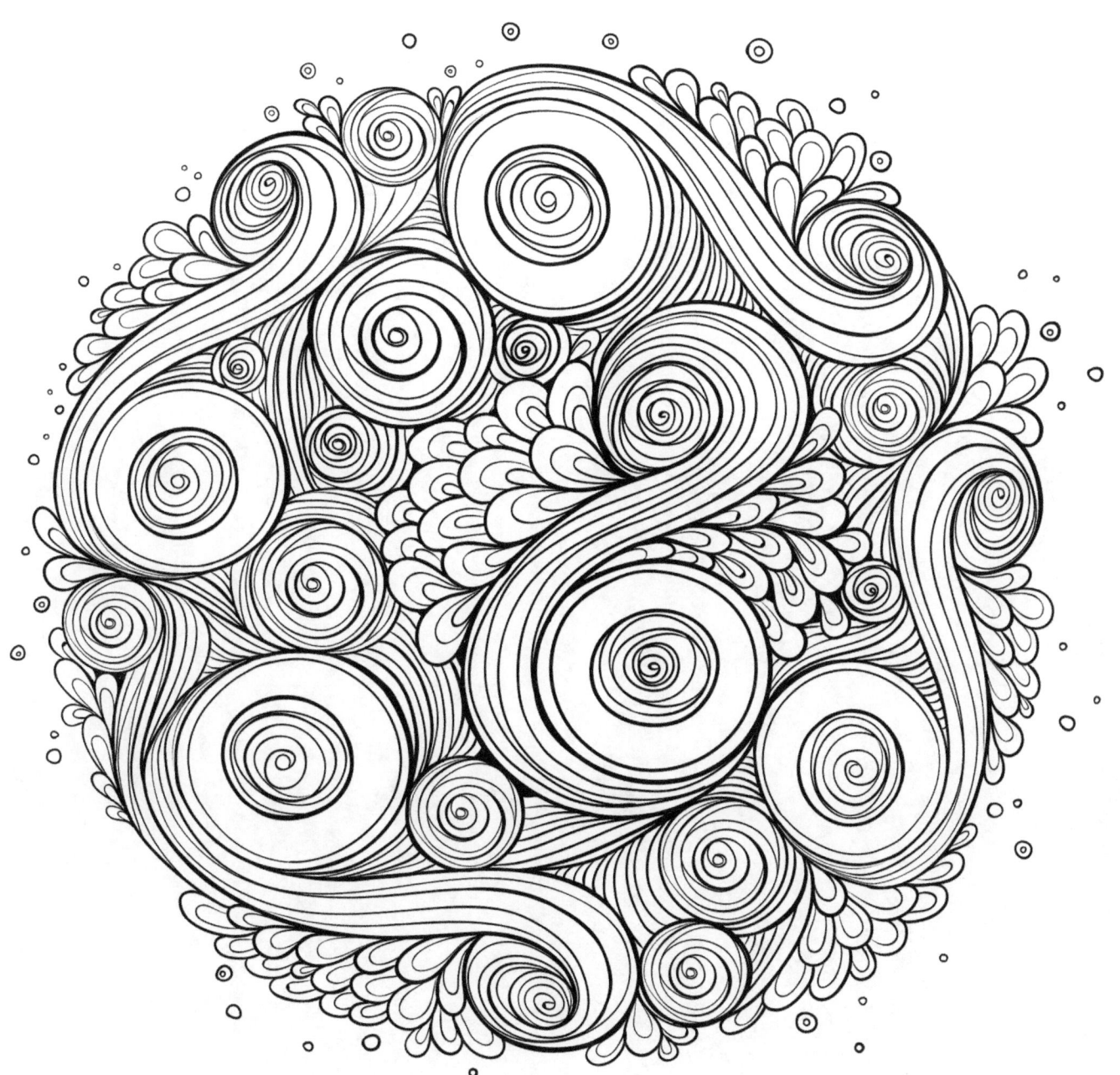

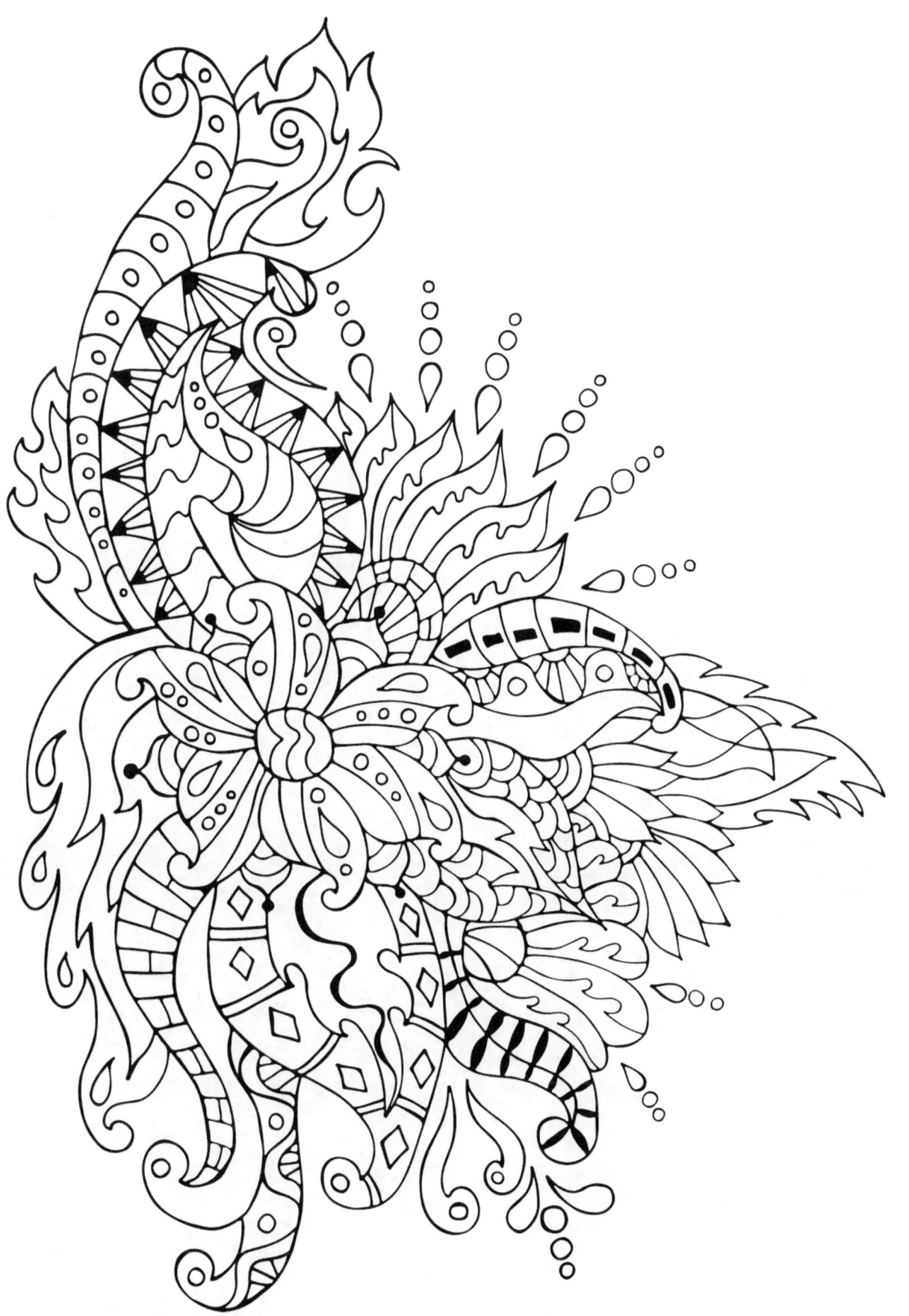

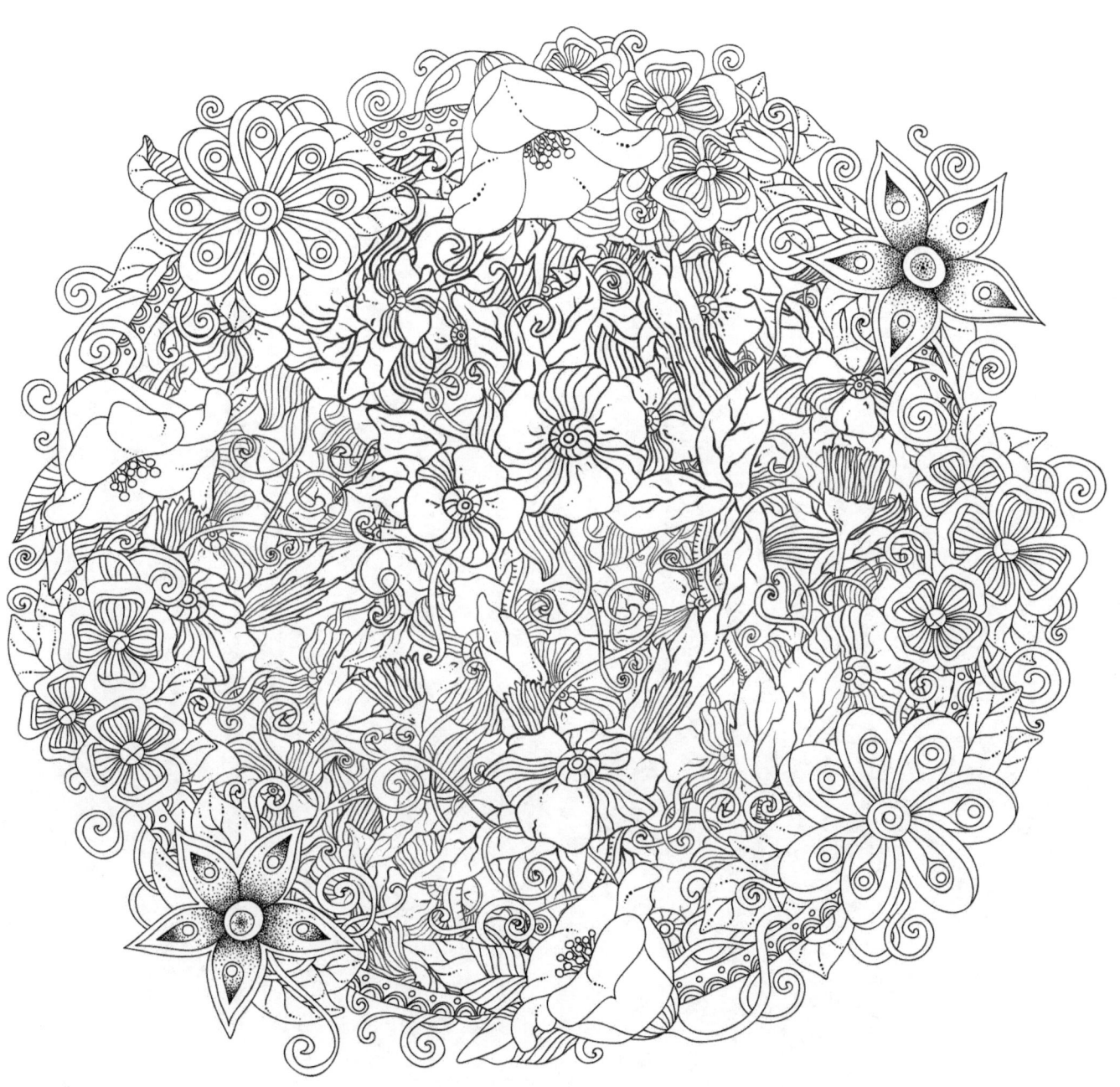

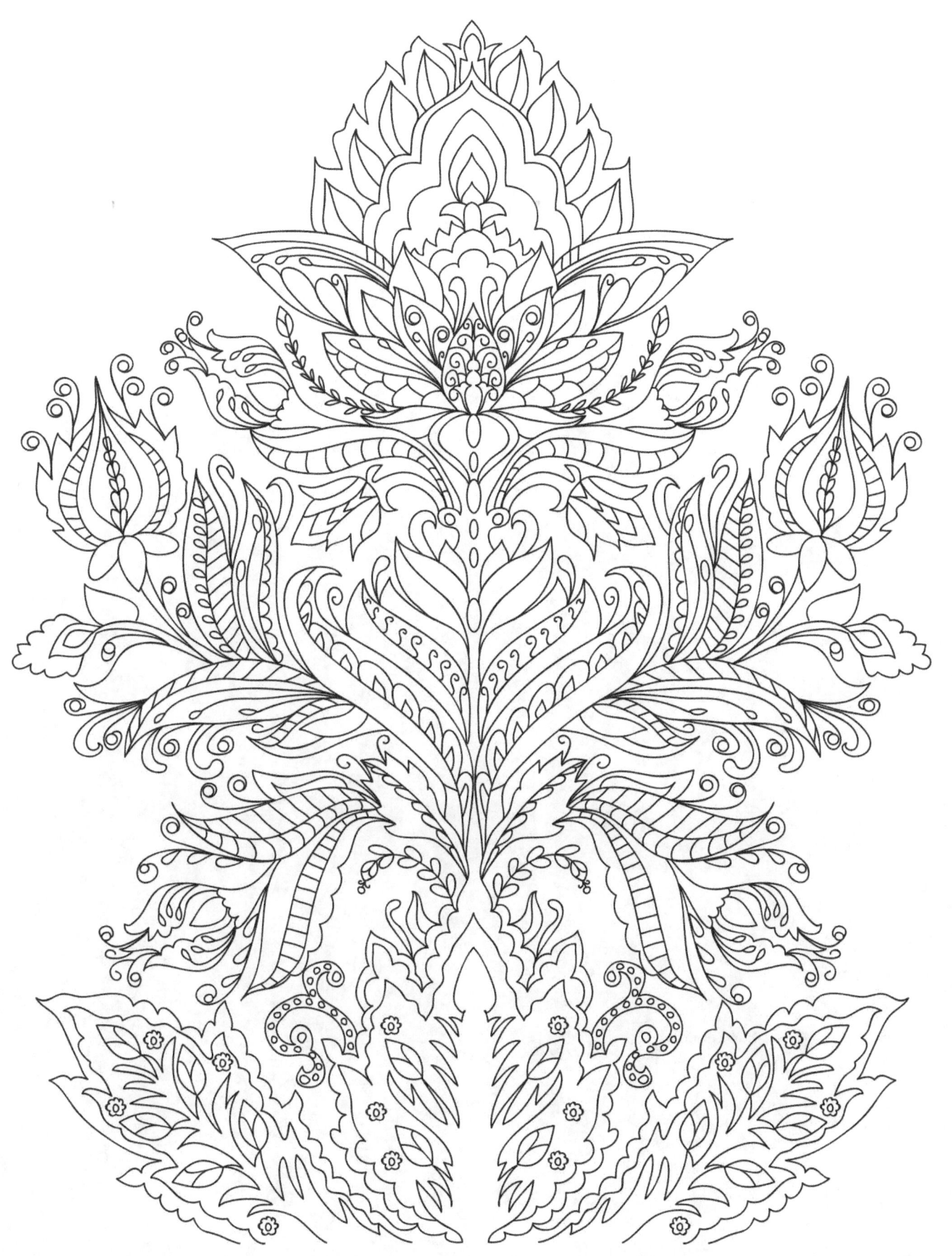

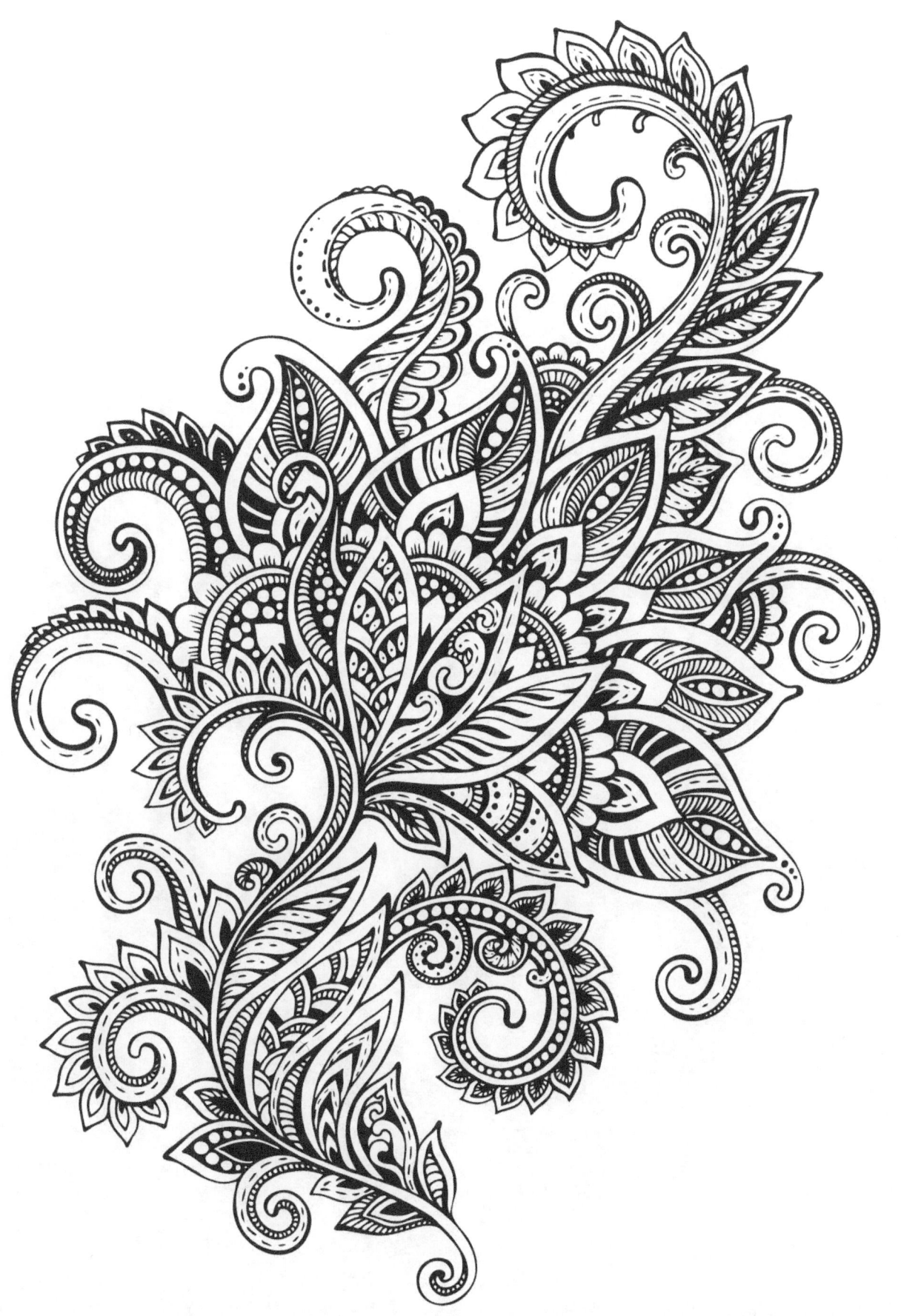

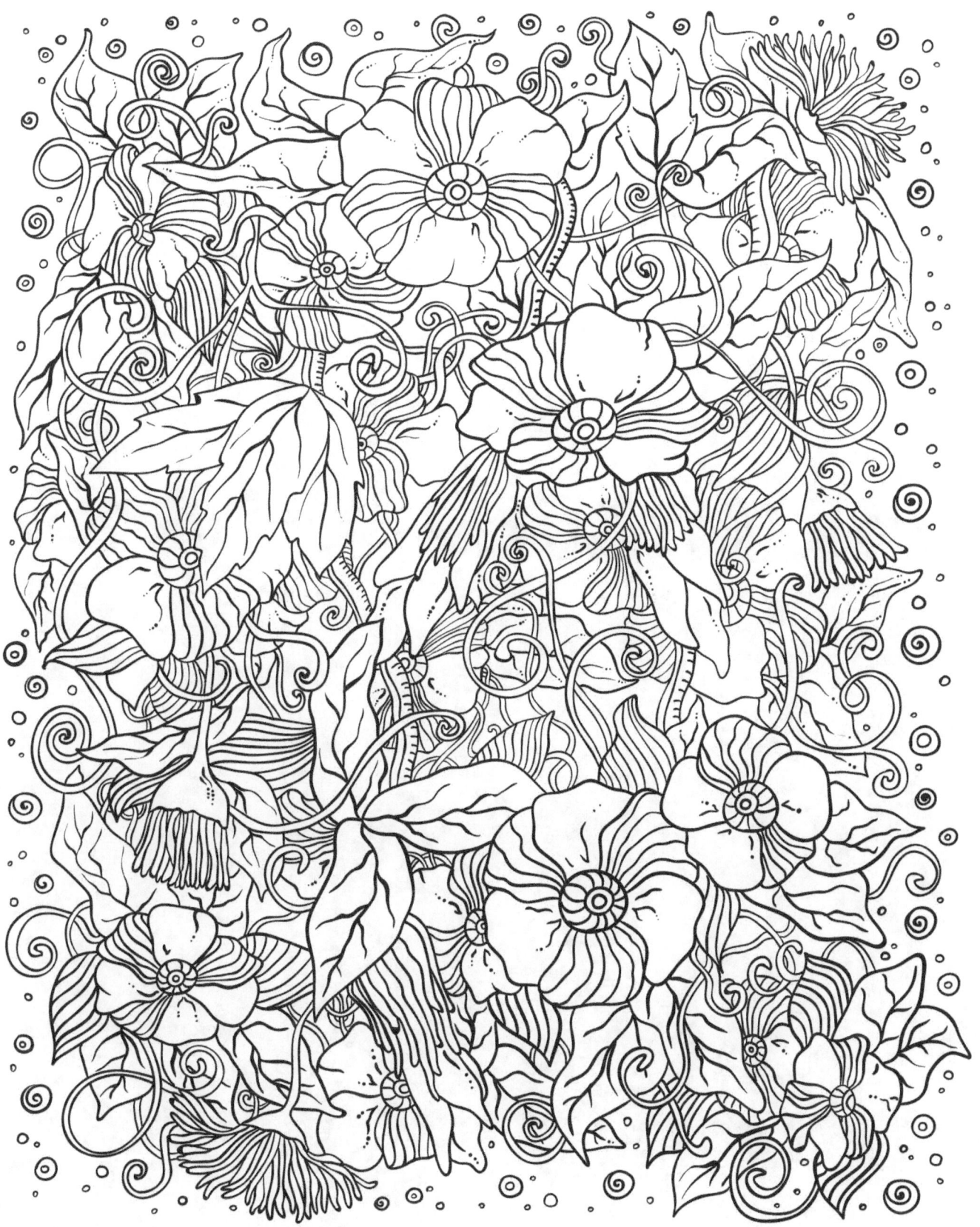

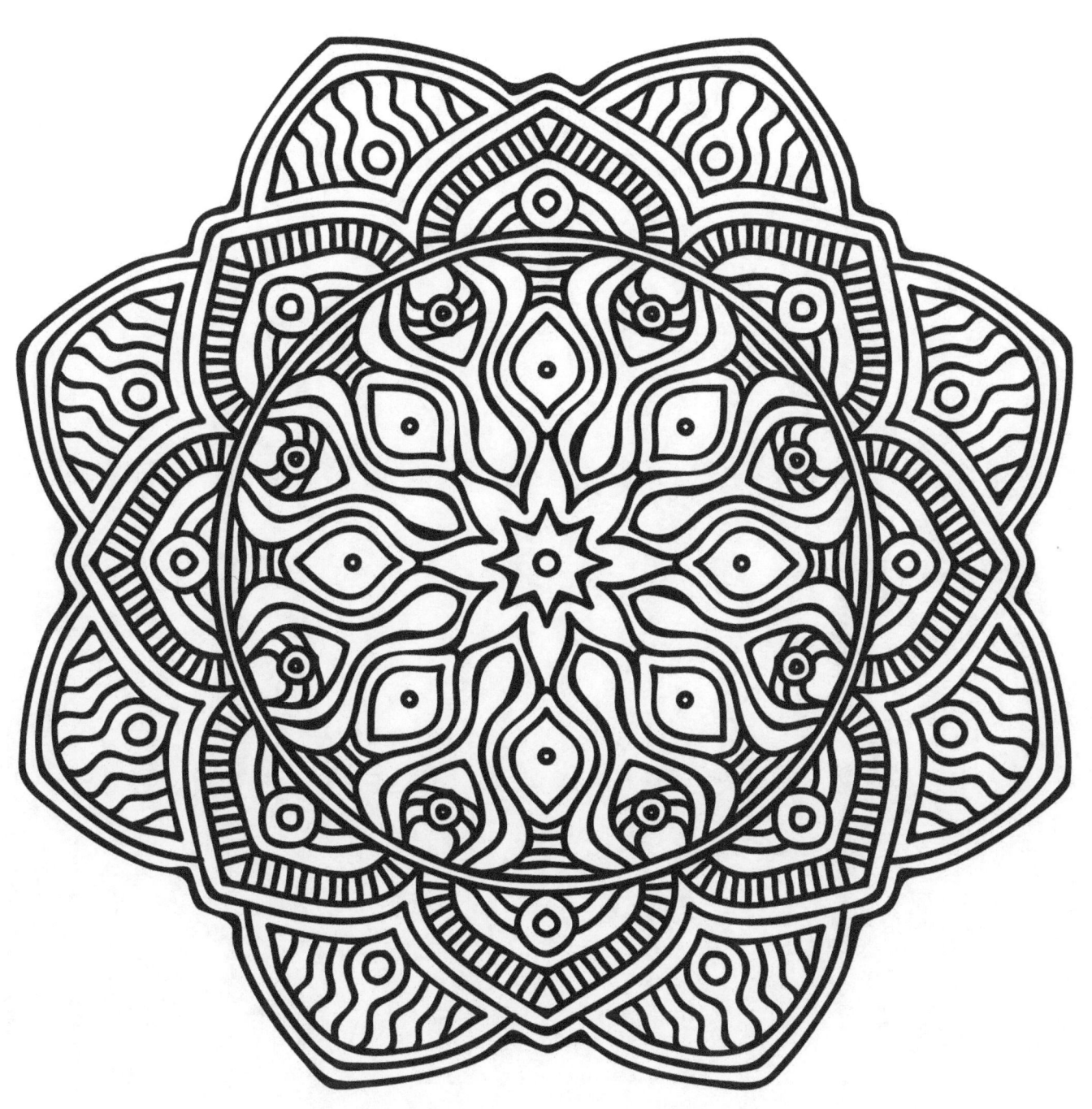

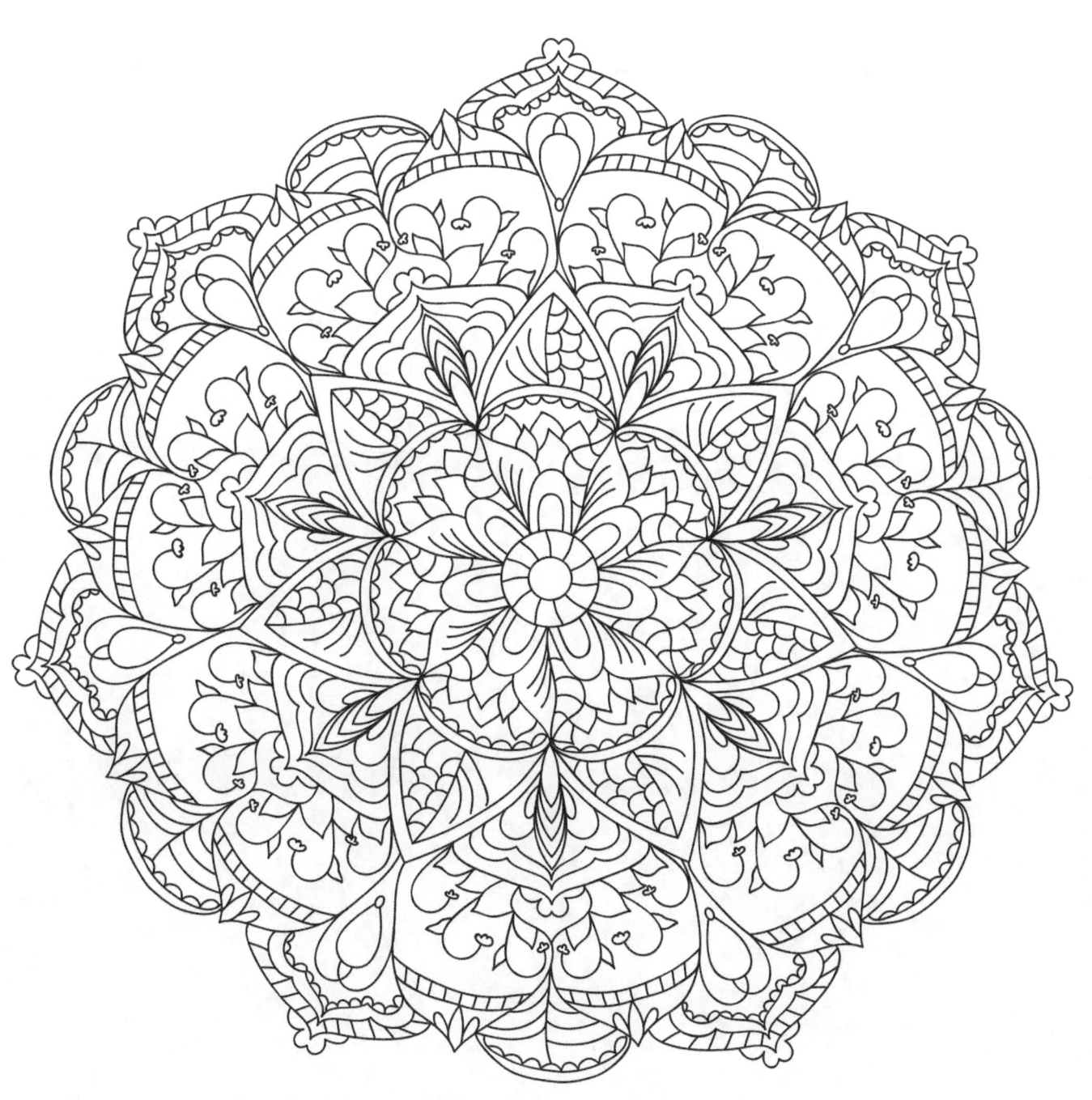

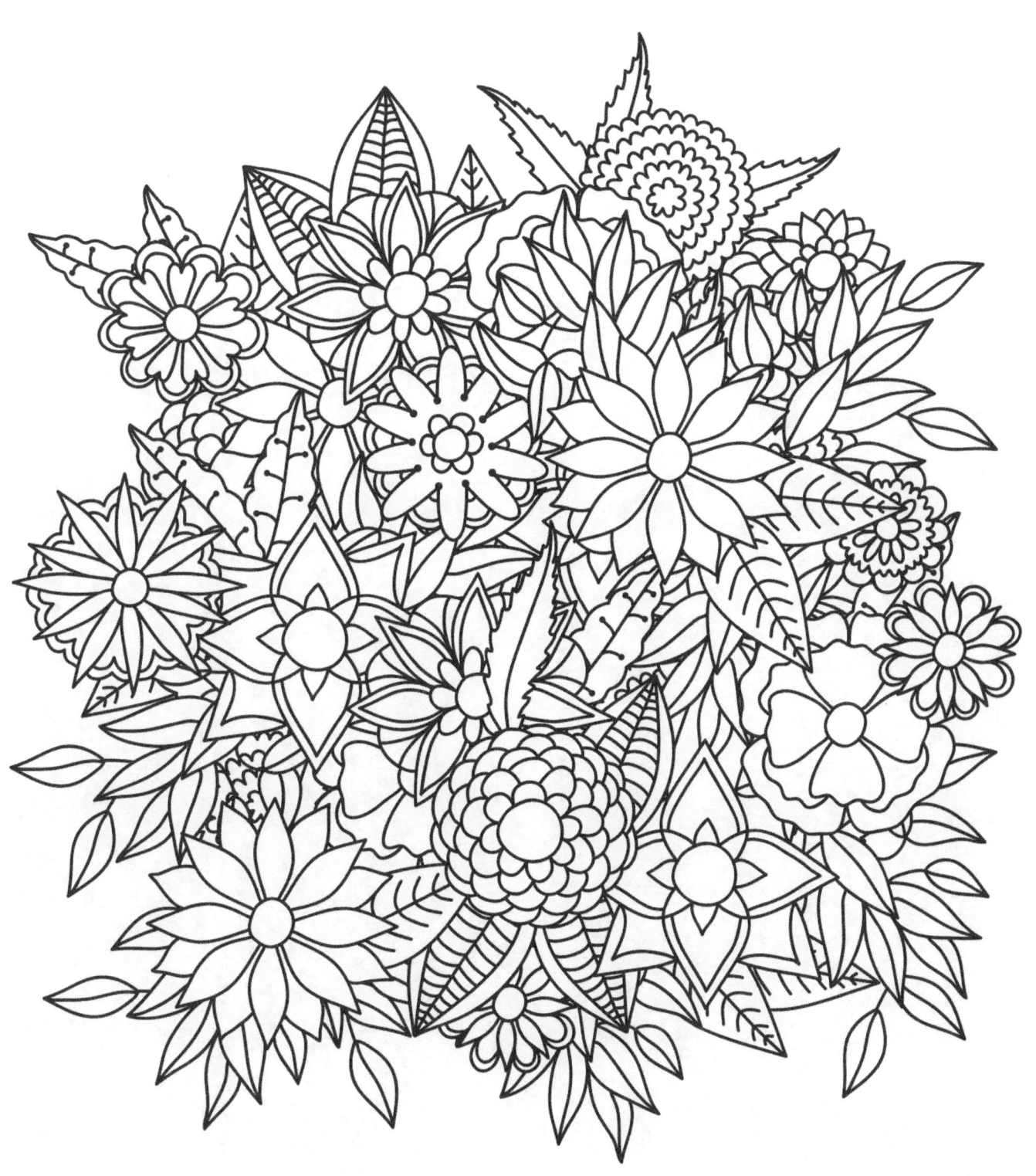

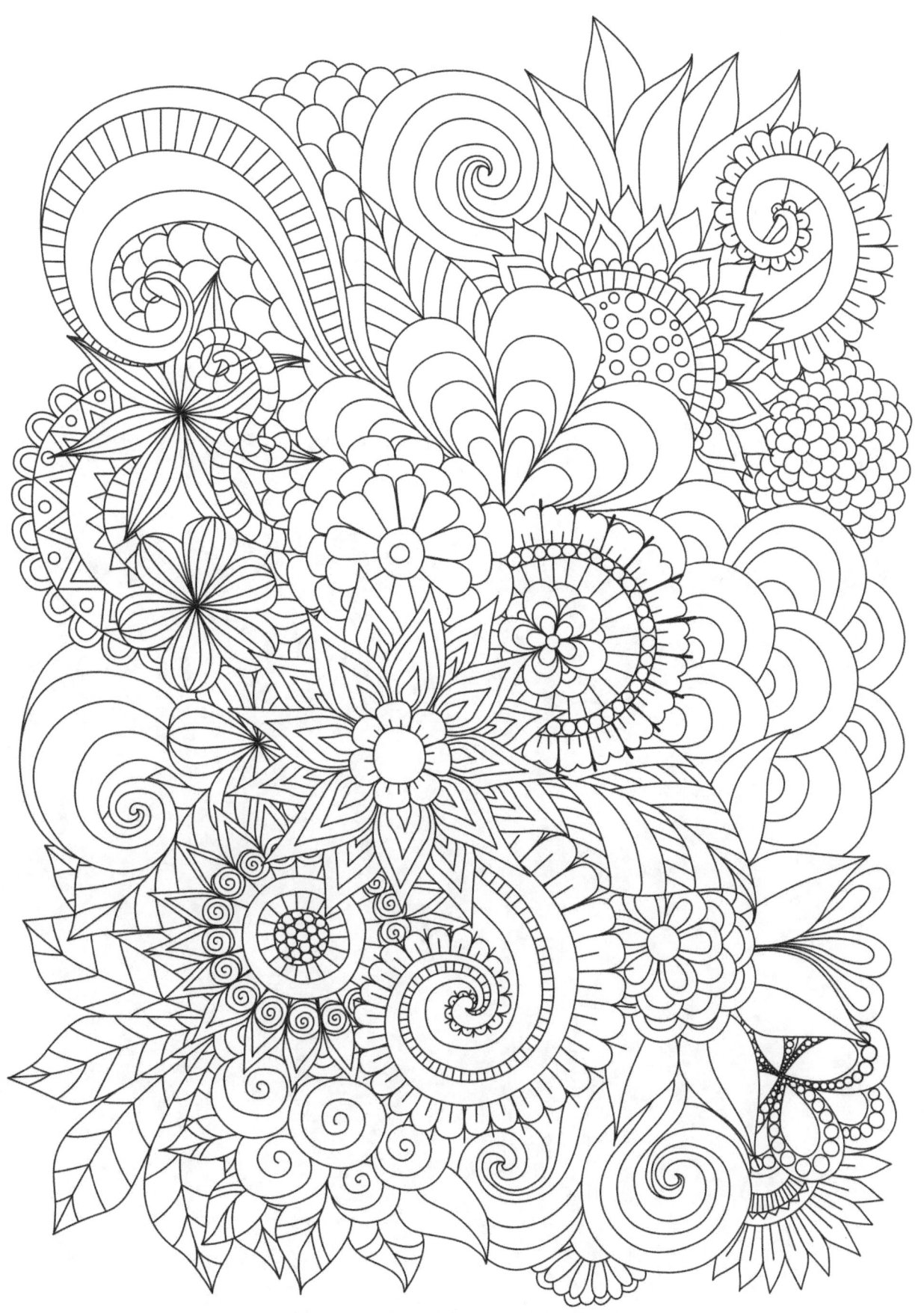

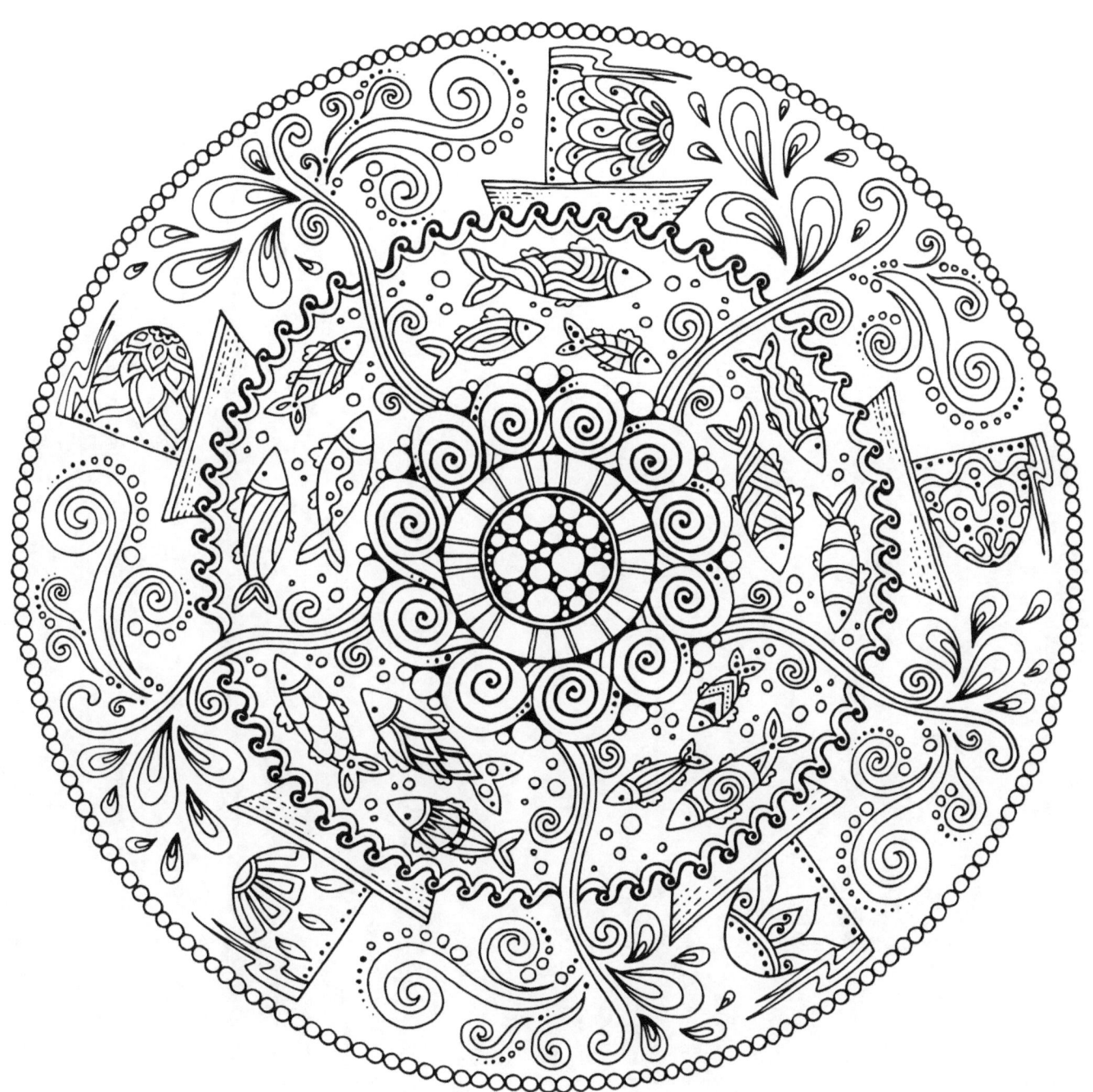

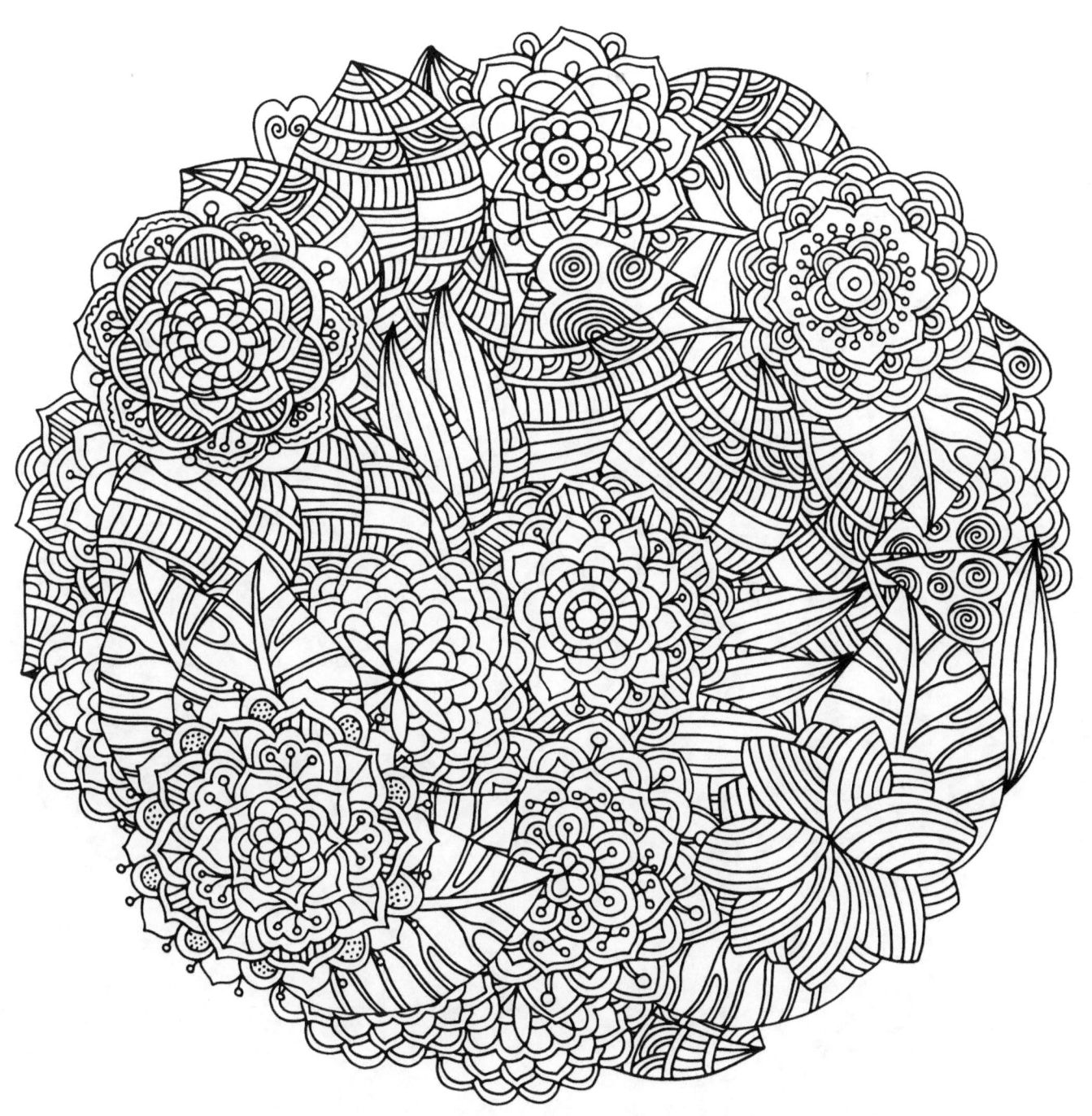

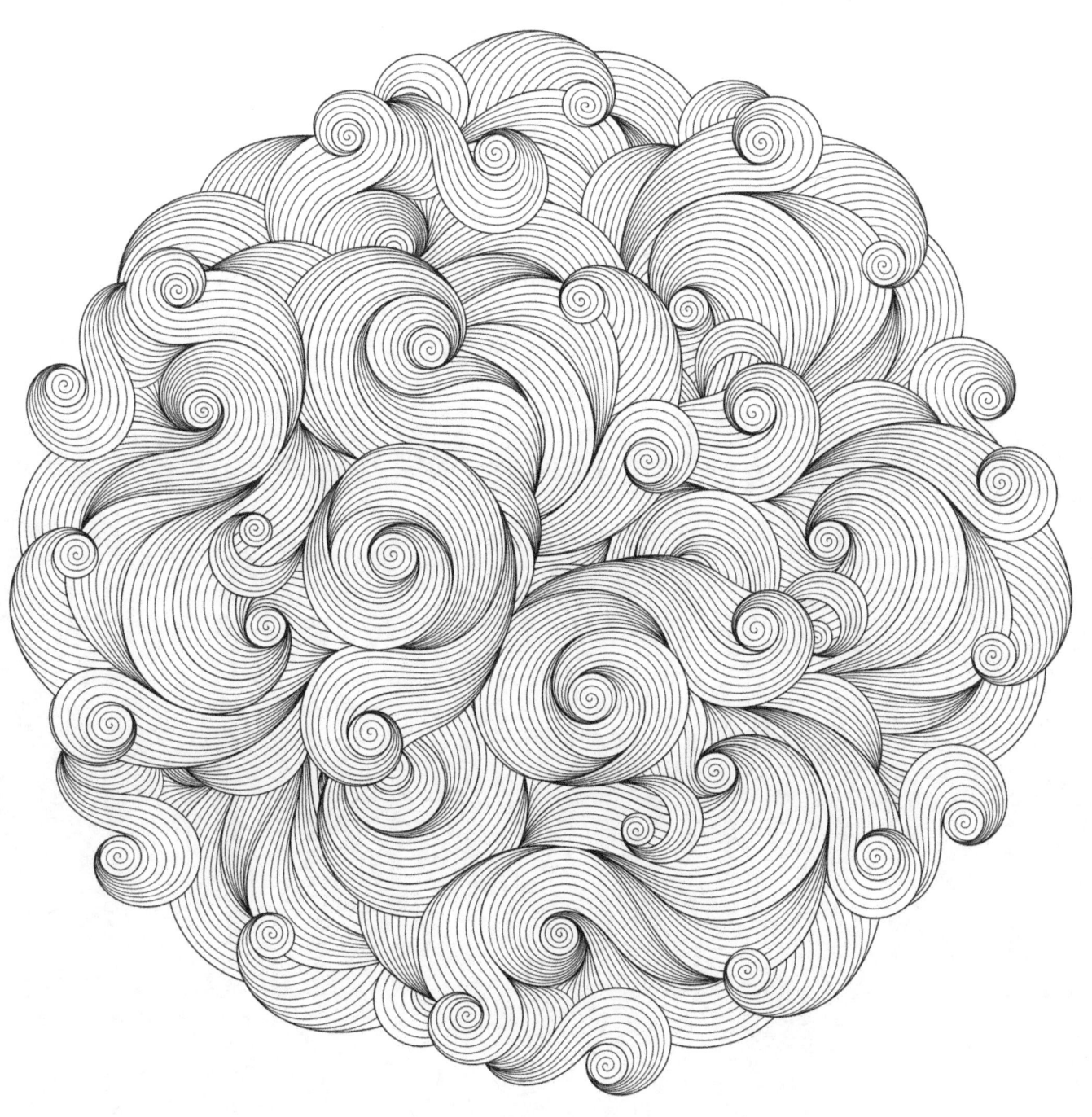

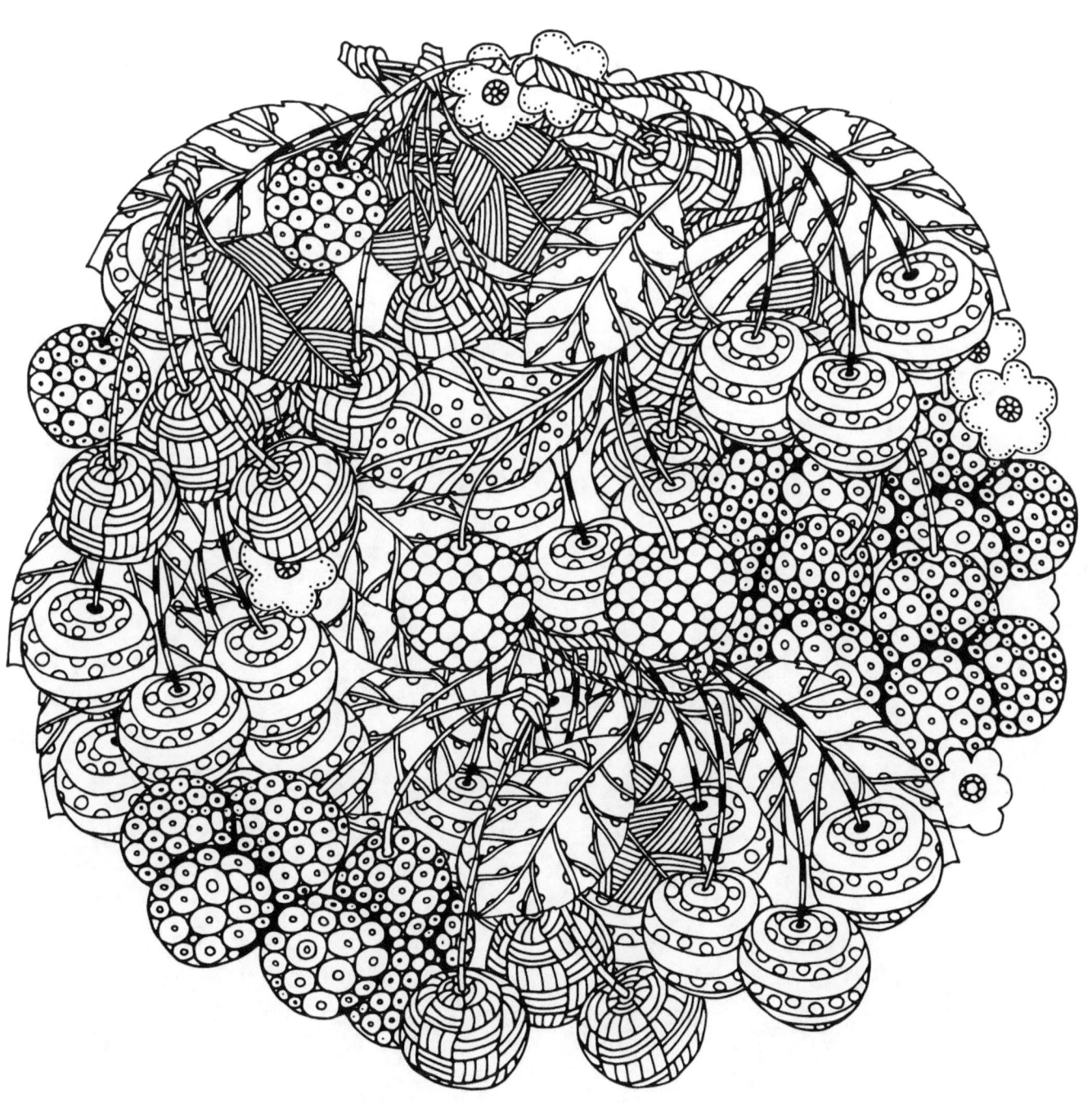

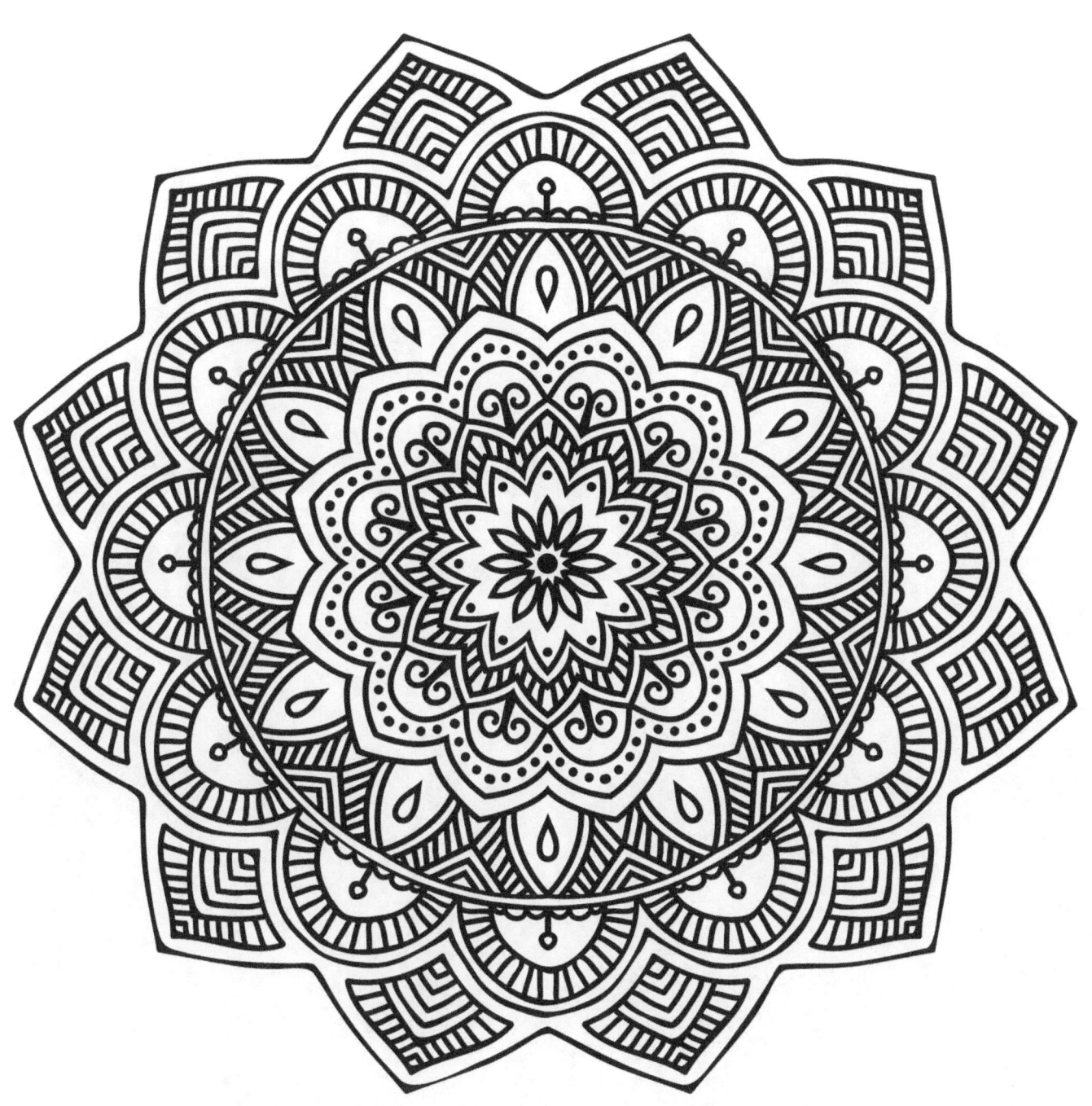

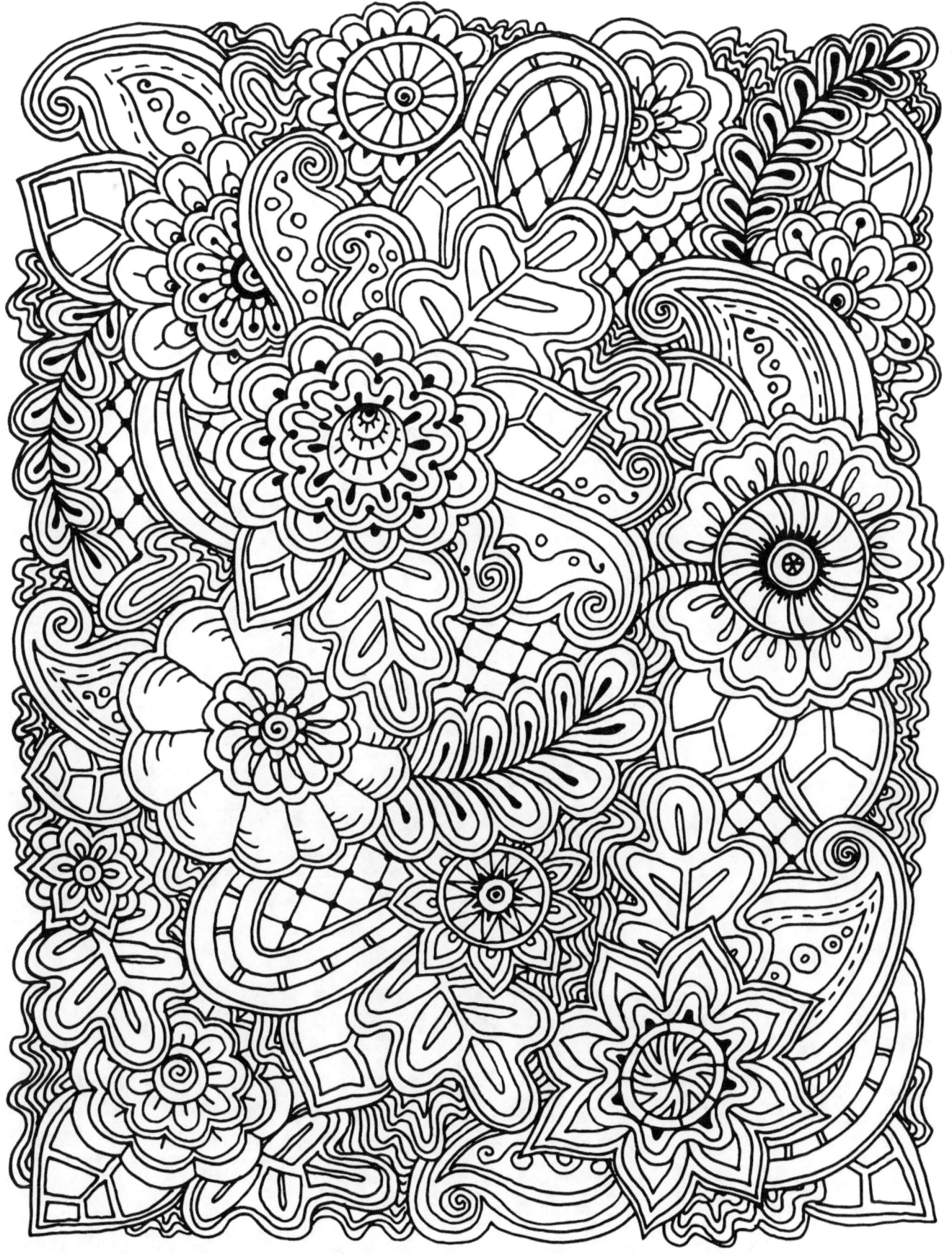

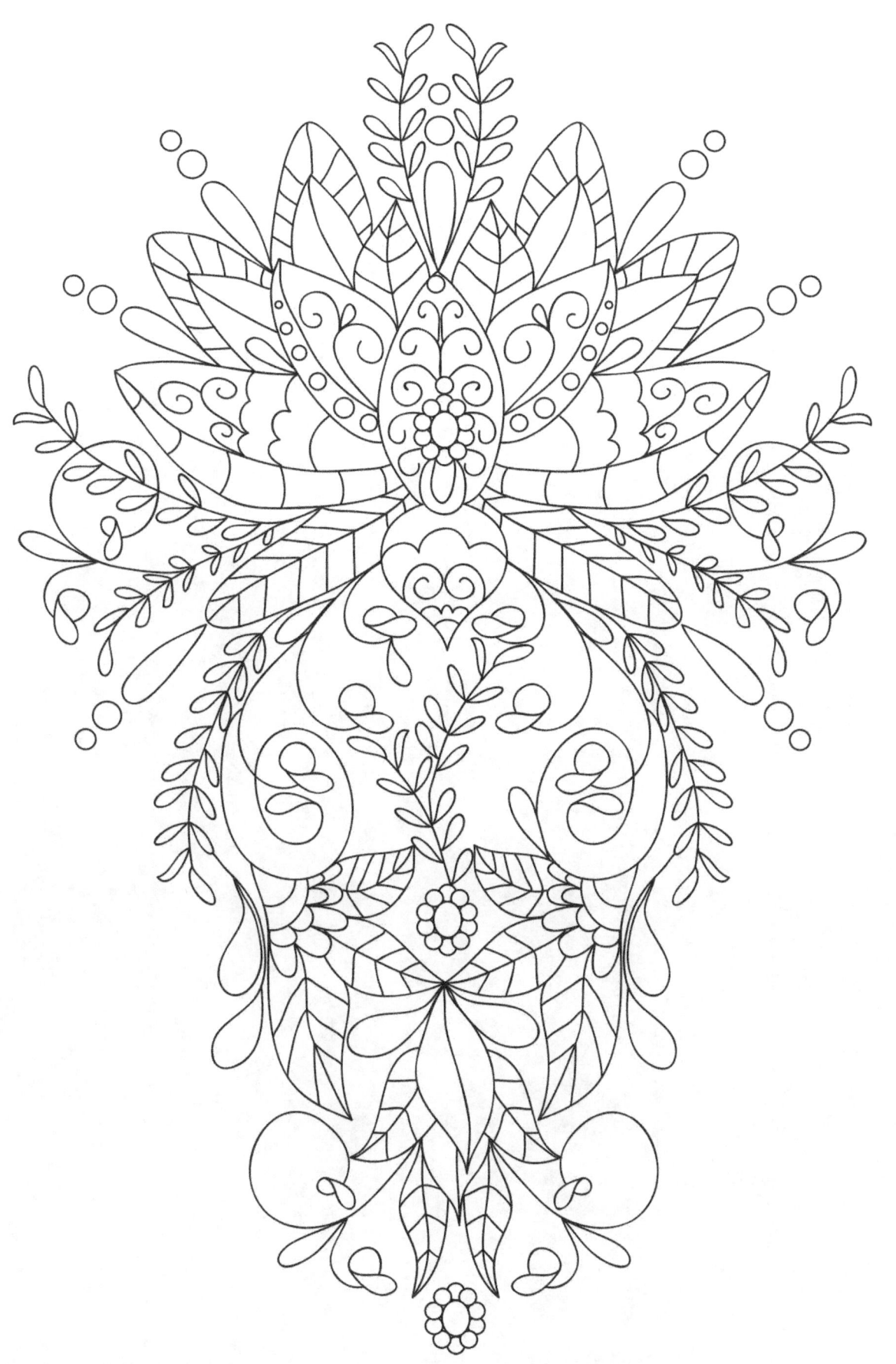

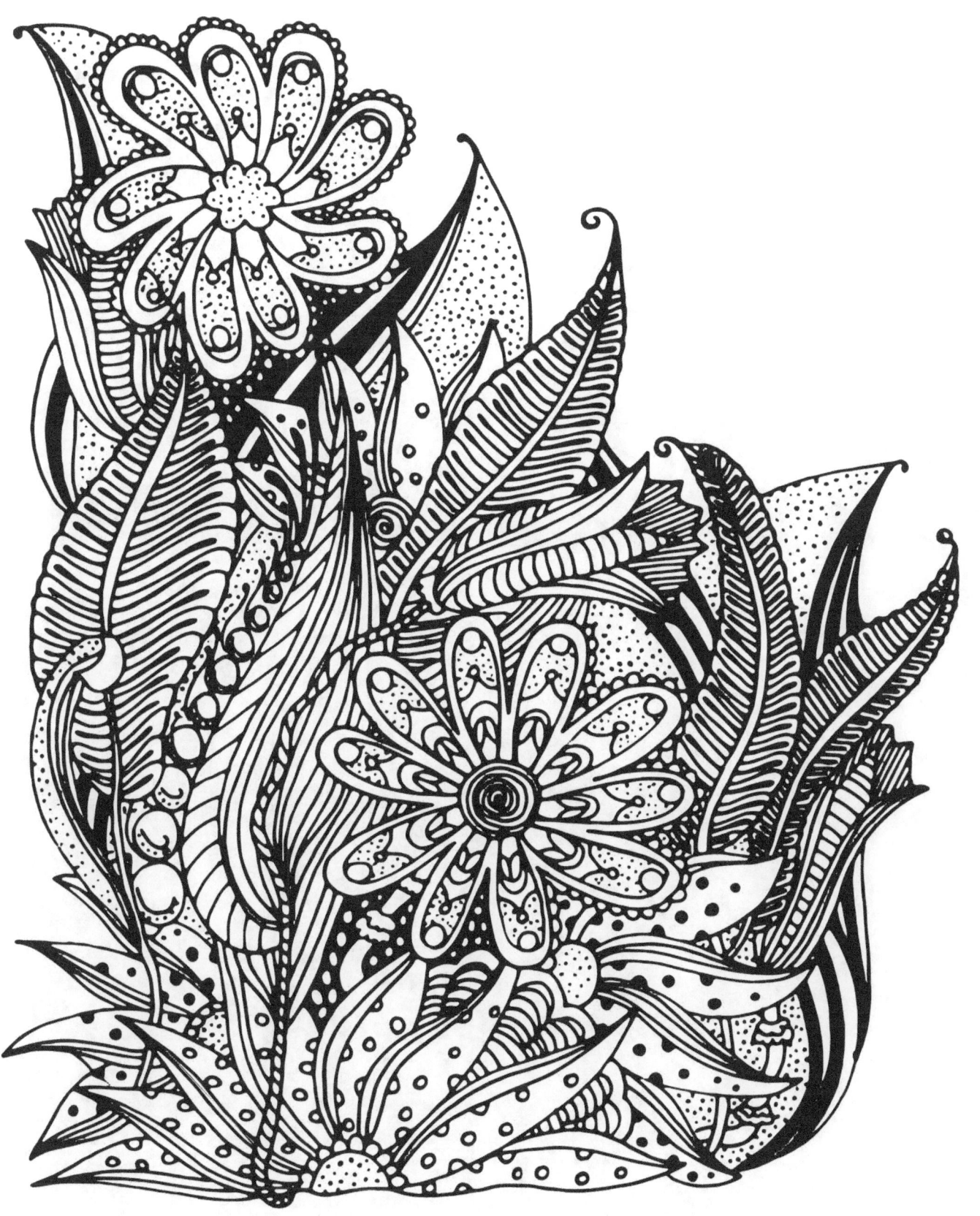

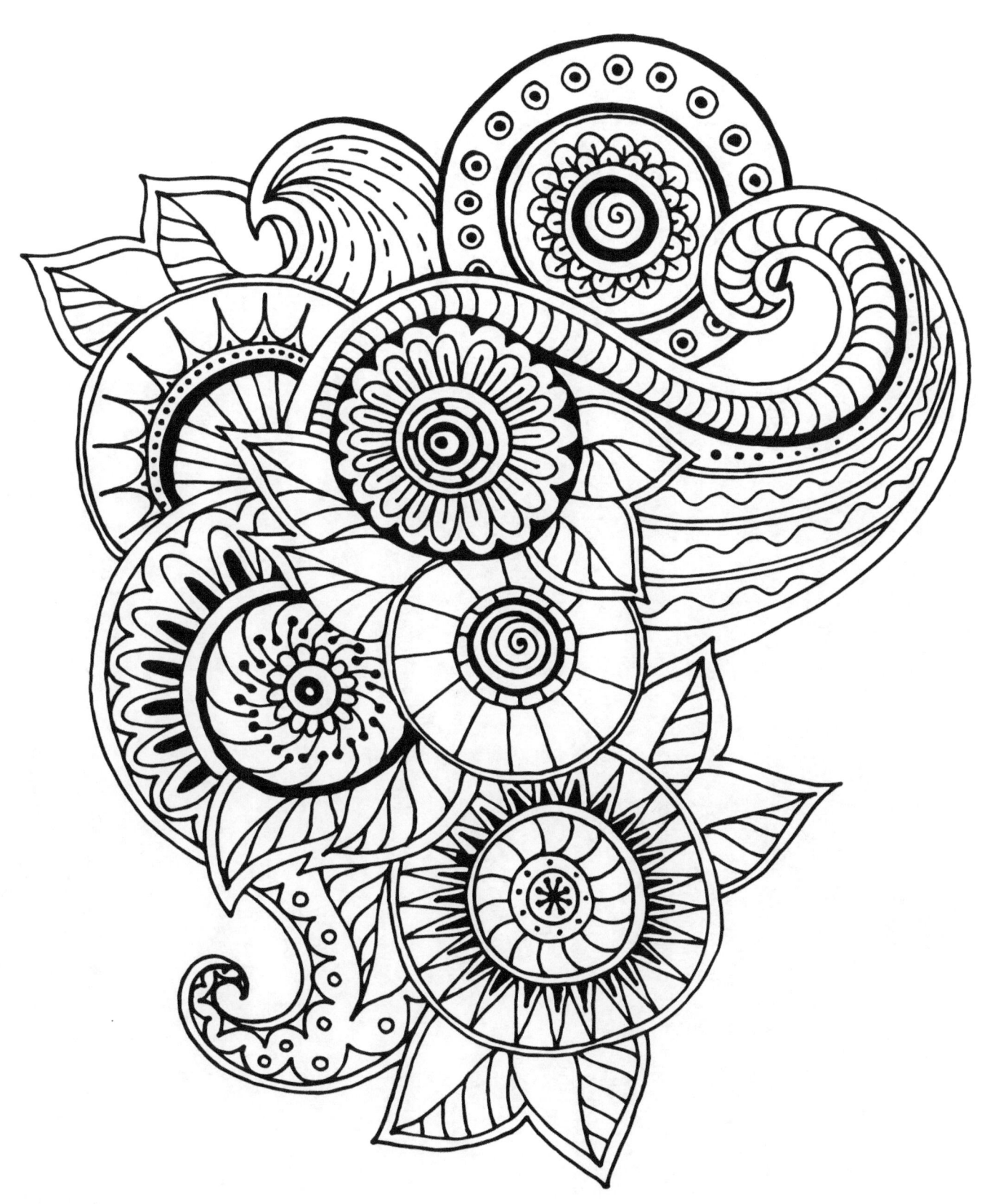

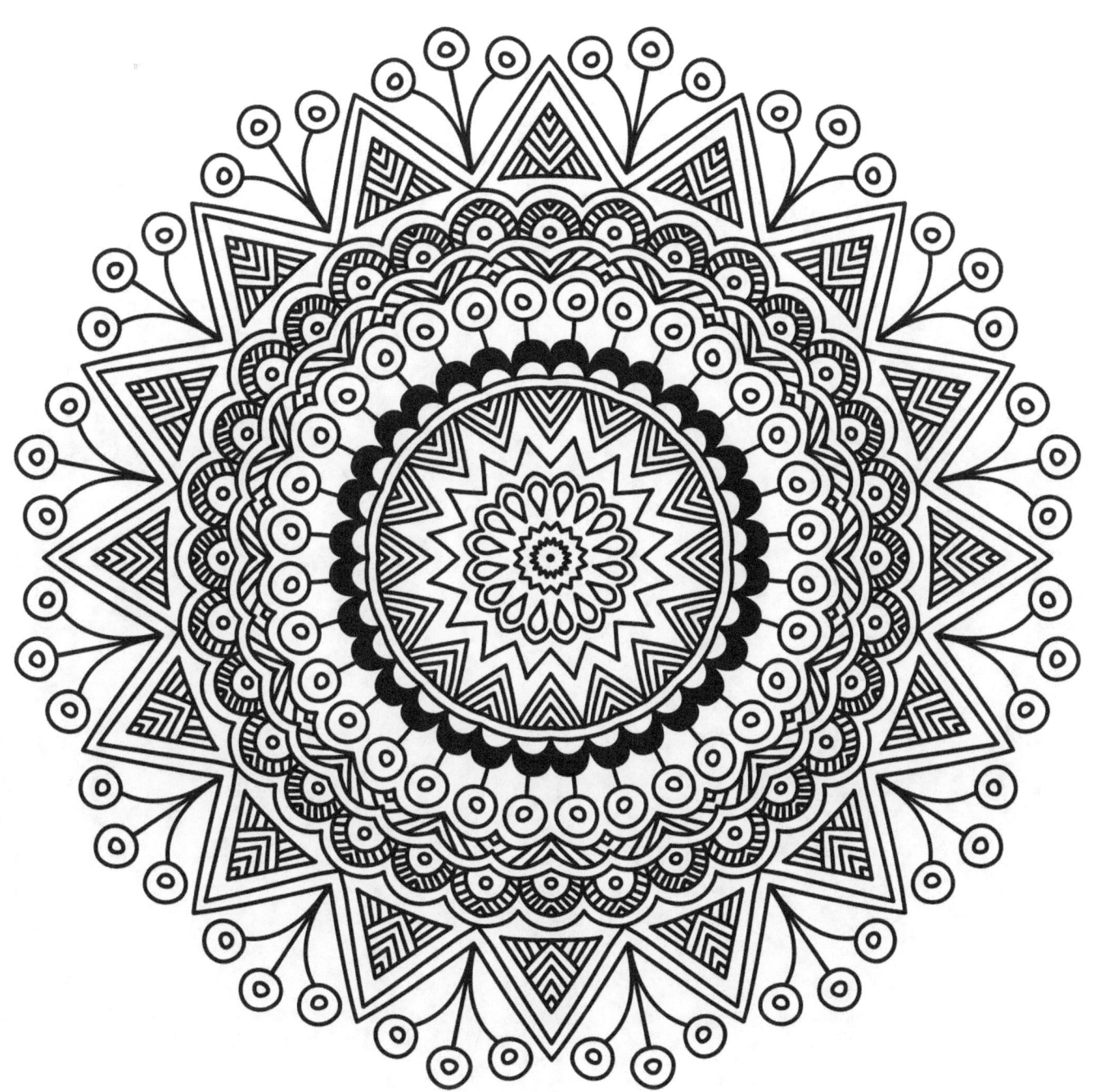

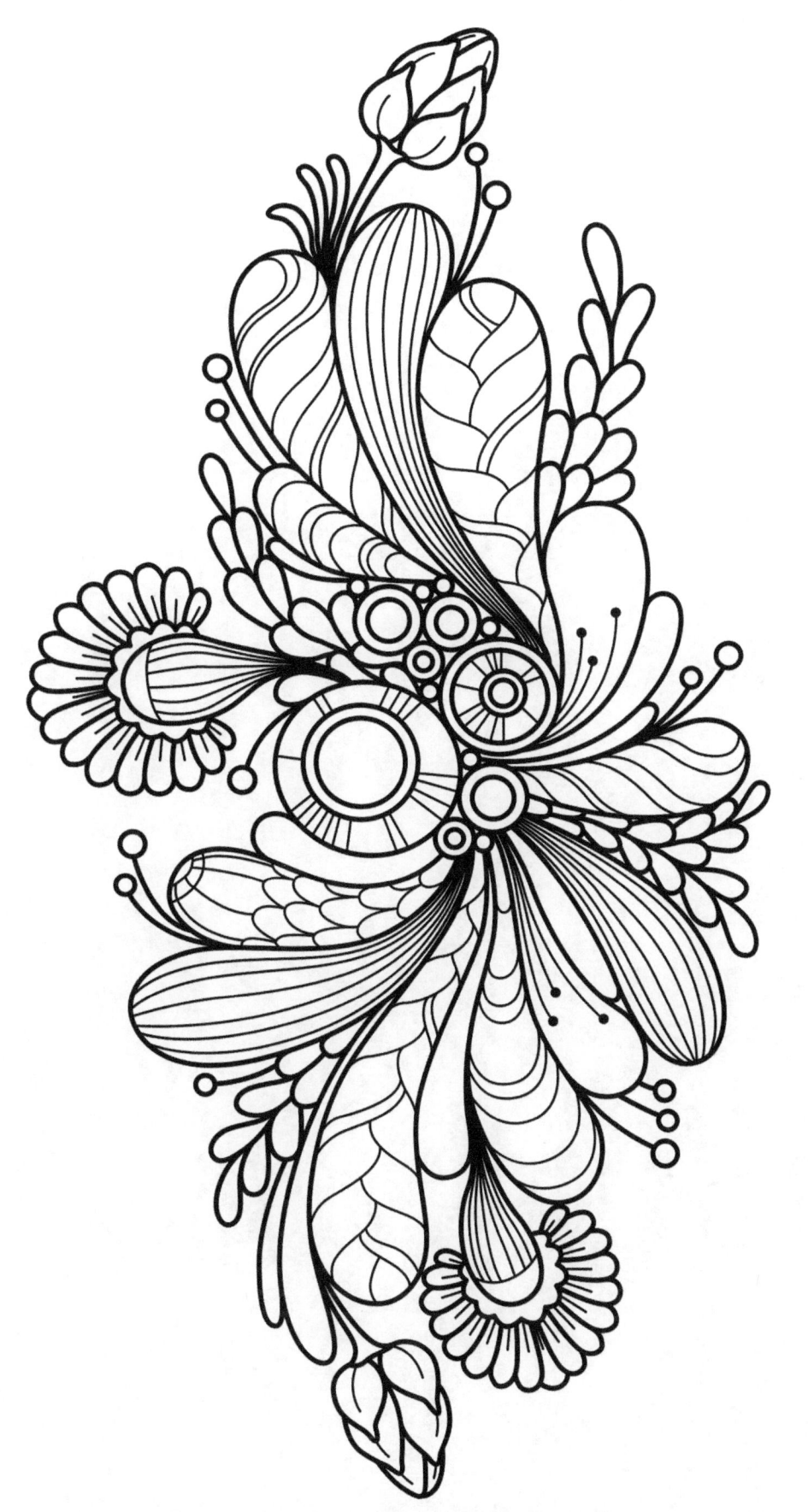

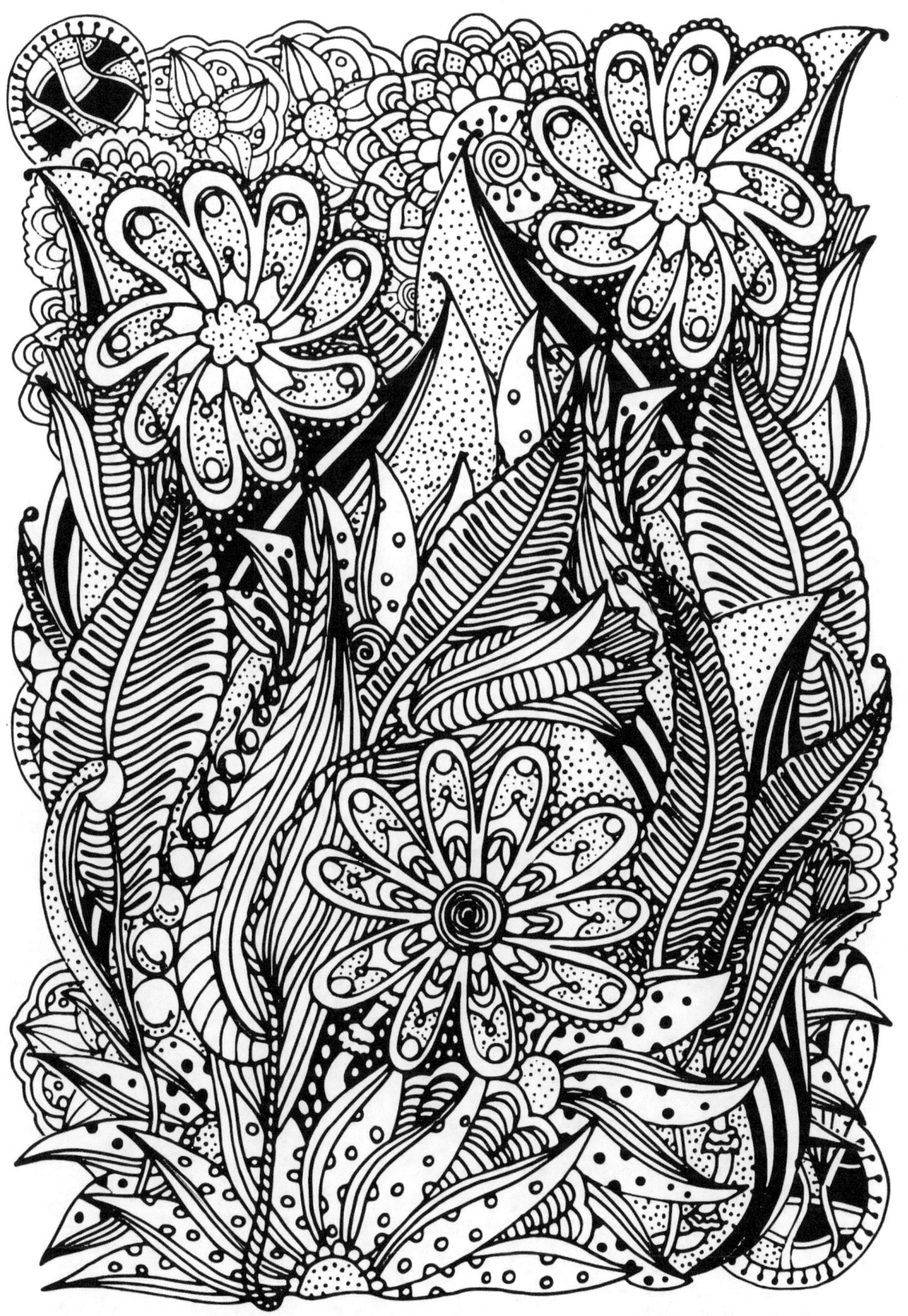

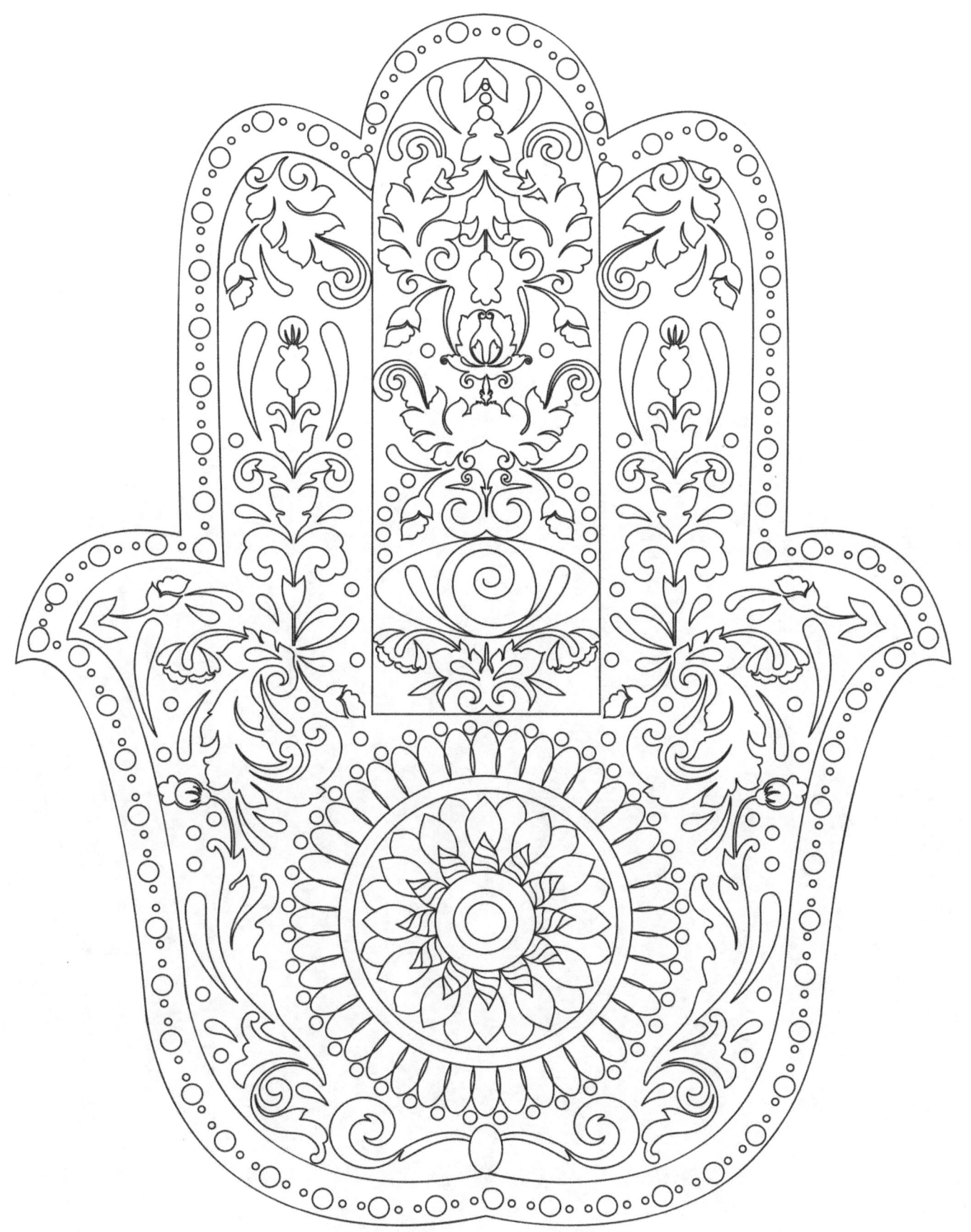

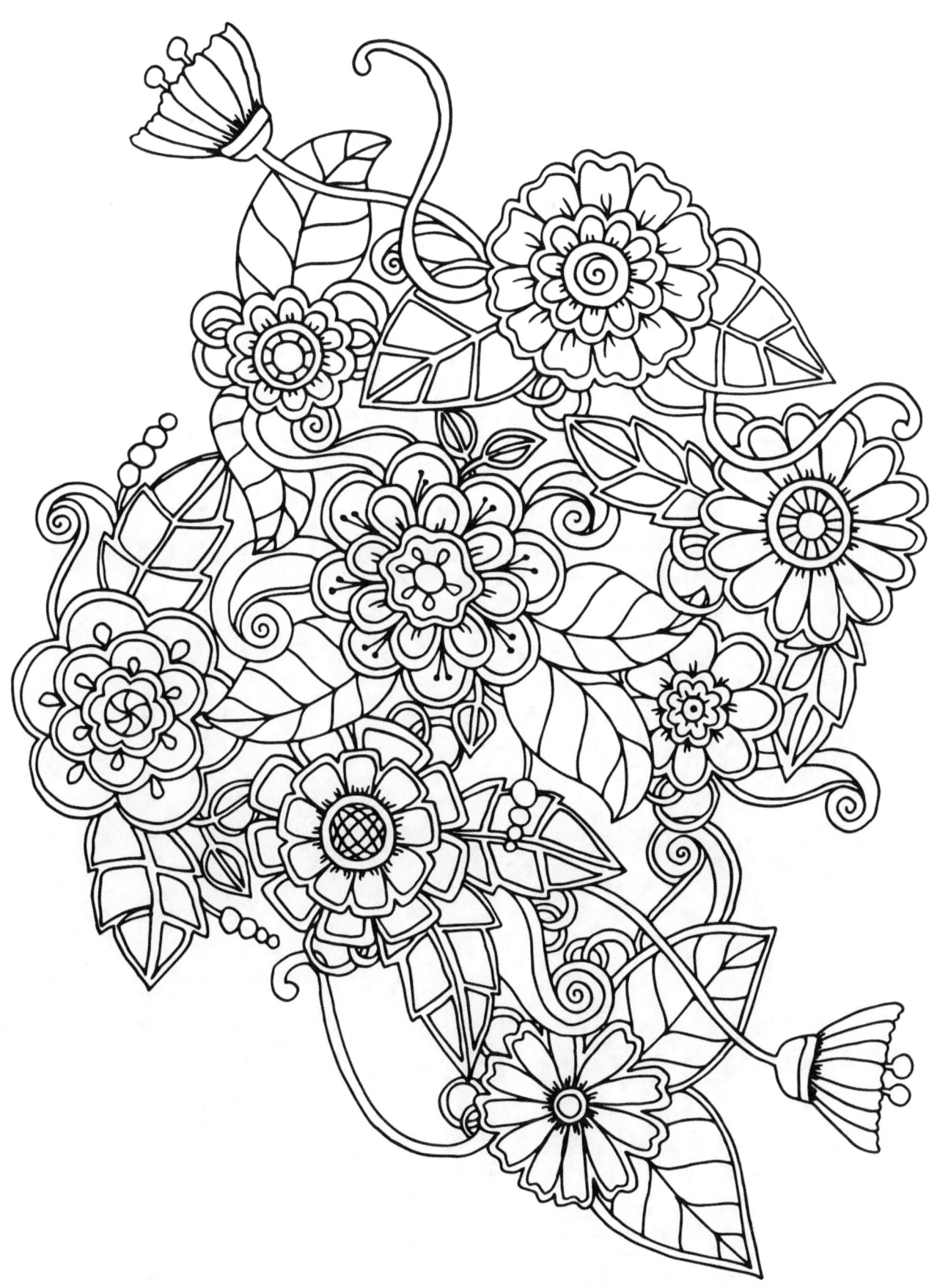

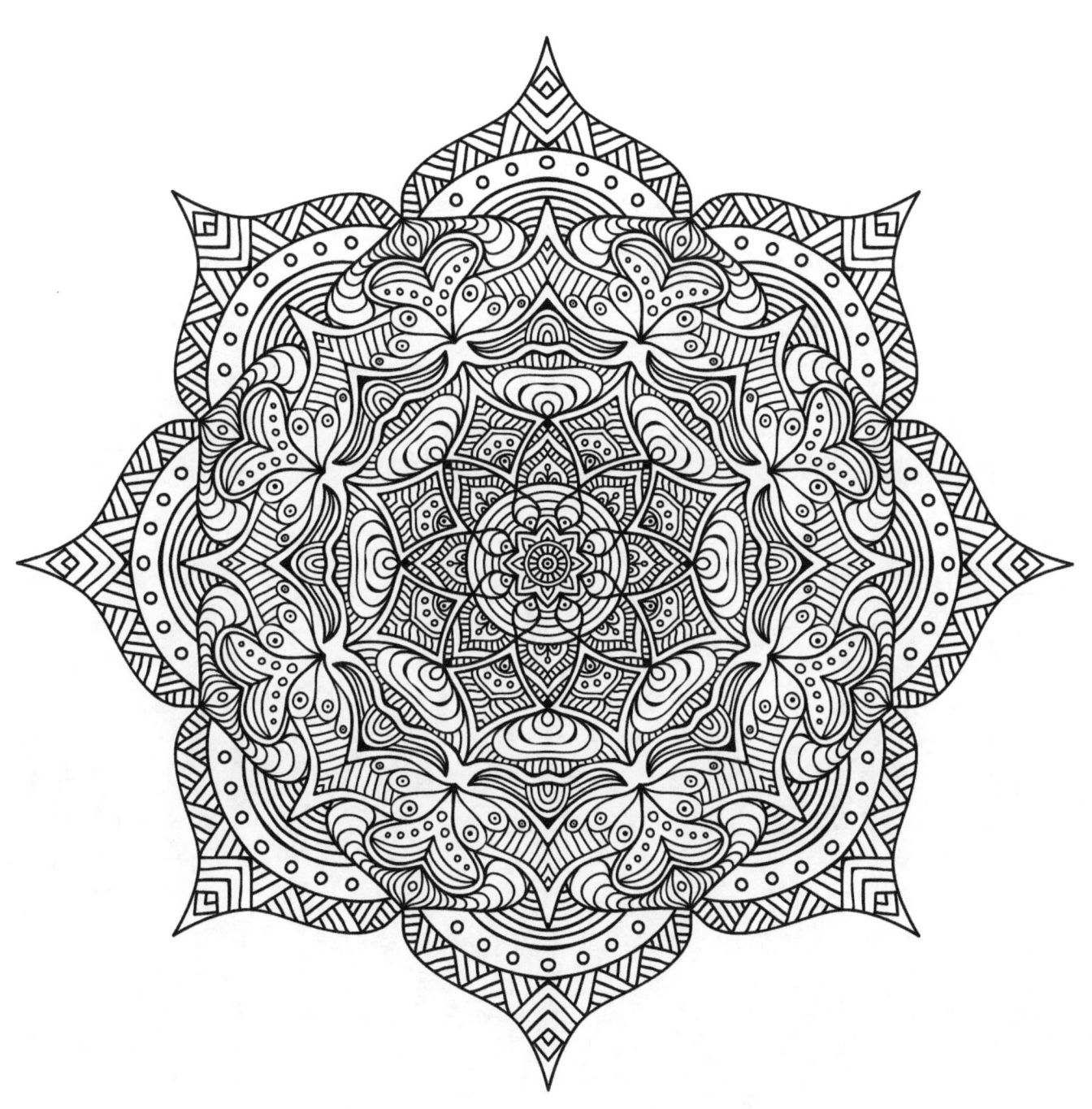

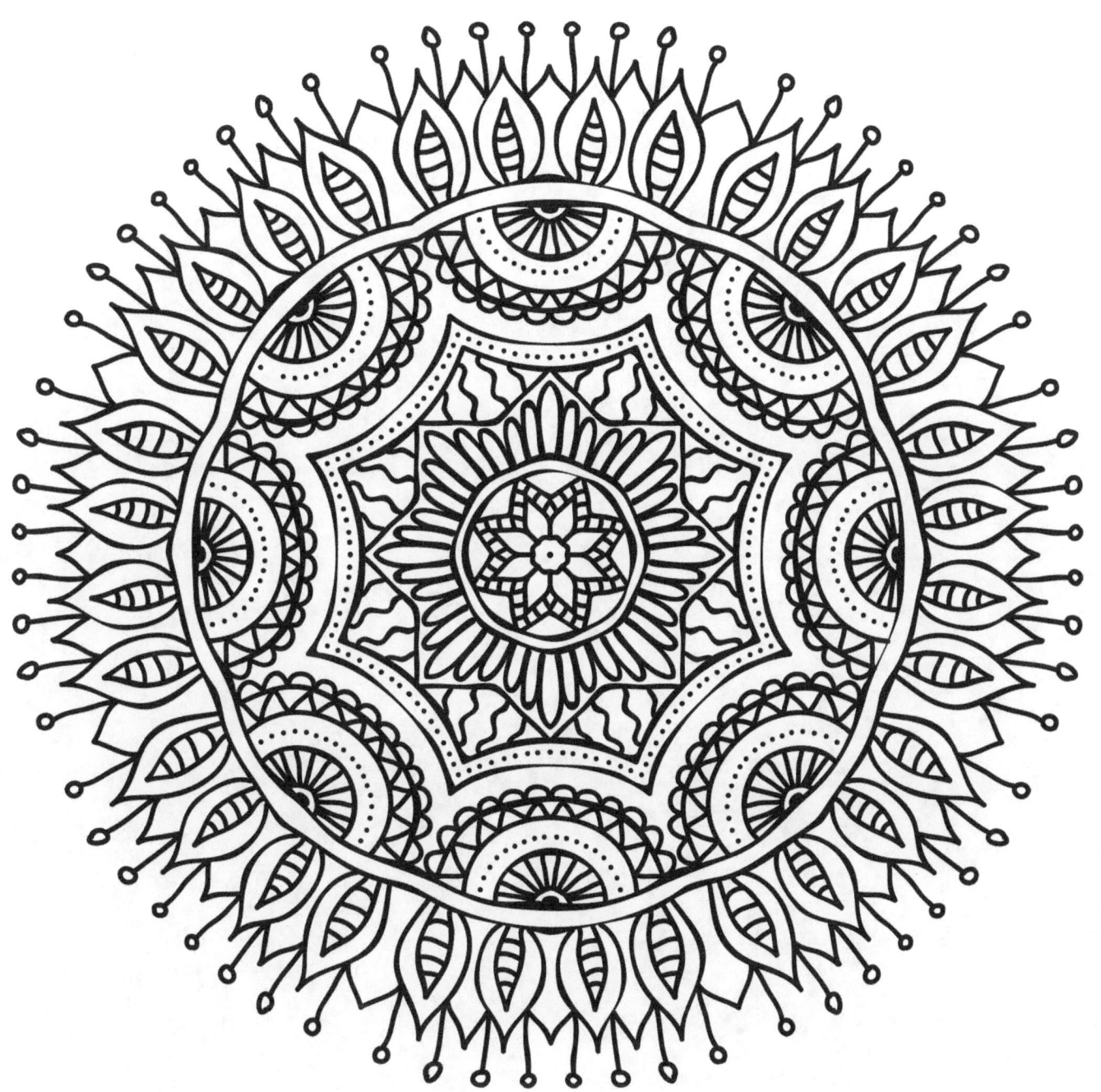

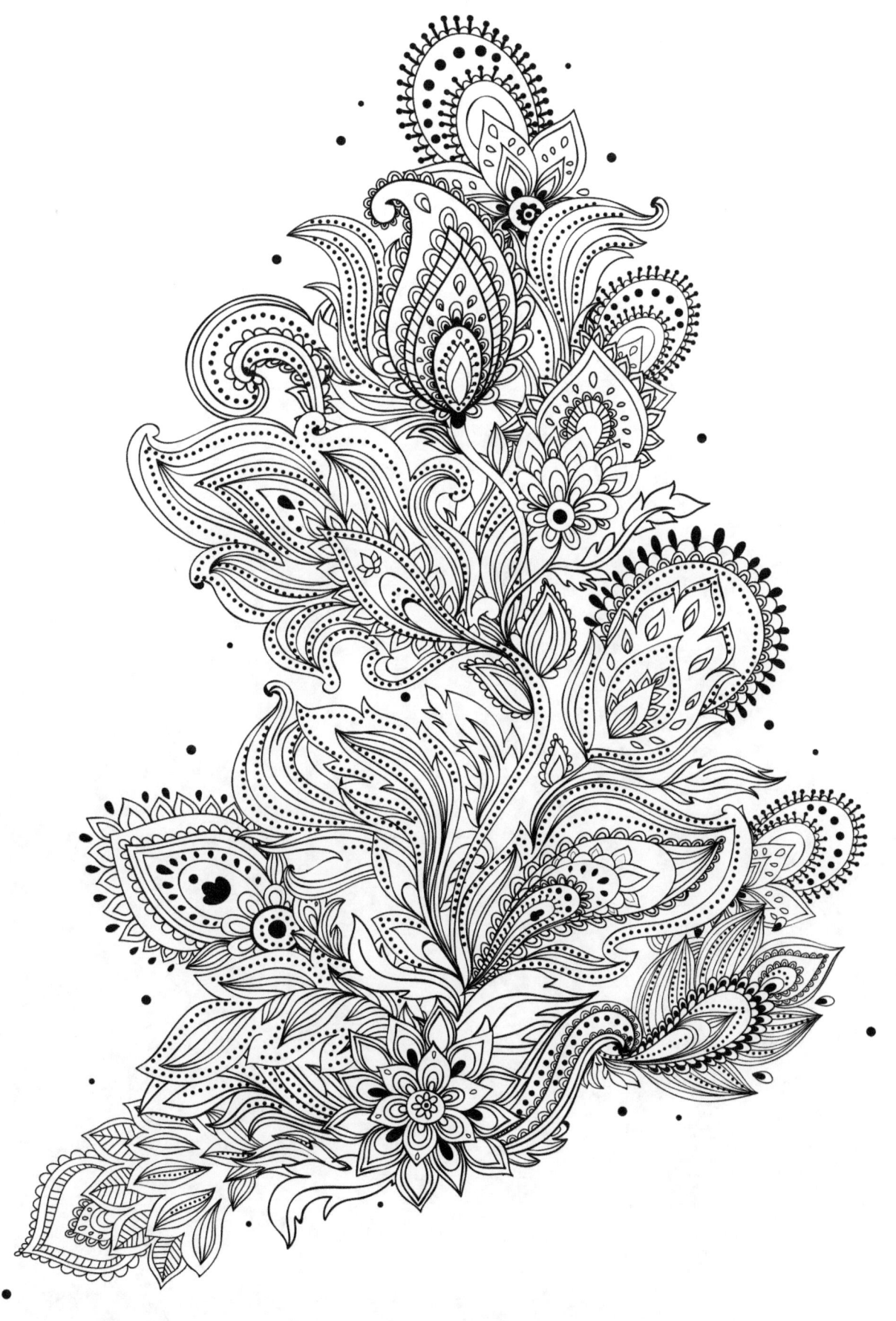

www.ingramcontent.com/pod-product-compliance
Lightning Source LLC
Chambersburg PA
CBHW080703190526
45169CB00006B/2227